QUEST FOR EXCELLENCE

An Adolescent's Guide To
Self-Confidence and Relationships

Lisa & Ranae,

Blossom so you
will grow in confidence
and be a blessing.

In His Joy,
Deborah Wueralin

Prov 3:13-18

QUEST FOR EXCELLENCE

An Adolescent's Guide To
Self-Confidence and Relationships

by
Deborah Wuerslin
with
Don H. Highlander, Jr., Ph.D.

Excellence Publishing

Stone Mountain, Georgia

QUEST FOR EXCELLENCE
Copyright © 1993 by Deborah Wuerslin.

Cover Design: Debbie Grimes
Cover Illustration: Mark James
Illustrations: Mark Herron

Printed in the United States of America.

This book is available at quantity discounts with bulk purchase for educational or business use. For information, please write to Excellence Publishing, P.O. Box 870853, Stone Mountain, Georgia 30087-0022.

About the Author

Deborah Wuerslin teaches the social and personal skills in this book to young people in private and public schools, in private homes, in department stores, and on retreats. She has adapted this course and successfully taught these skills to Special Ed. students in the public school system.

As a wife of 22 years and homemaker, she has devoted her life to her family and volunteered thousands of hours in her church, her children's schools, and in her community. Church and school officials often call upon her to set up programs because of her leadership and organizational abilities. She teaches Sunday school and speaks at church, women's clubs, and community functions. Her family also keeps her busy and humble by constantly talking her into attempting a new sport. Tennis, camping, and hiking are her favorite activities. Ice skating, she's learning. Skiing and rock climbing keep her in a constant state of terror.

About the Editor

Dr. Highlander is a licensed psychotherapist, writer, teacher, clinical supervisor and ordained minister who serves as director of the Northlake Counseling Center, a private practice clinic in Atlanta, Georgia. He has led numerous seminars on leadership training, parenting, group counseling, parent-teacher education and family life. He is author of the best seller, PARENTS WHO ENCOURAGE, CHILDREN WHO SUCCEED (Tyndale House Publishers) which deals with parenting, personal growth, marriage enrichment and communication skills.

Although most of the materials for this book have been researched, compiled and taught by Mrs. Deborah Wuerslin, Dr. Highlander supplied many practical insights and applications throughout. He also encouraged her to write, and teach these materials in schools, churches and Christian organizations in the metro Atlanta area.

DEDICATION

My family -- Tom, Diane, Paul, and Mark.
Your enthusiastic support in all of my endeavors
continues to bless me.

My parents -- Herb and Gerry Whyte.
Thank you for teaching me how to be a lady
and for your example in sharing your skills and God-given talents with
others.

ACKNOWLEDGMENTS

Family therapists, pastors, friends, and parents persuaded me to write a book that could be used as a tool for parents. Teens and younger girls and boys asked me to write a book they could understand and one that would capture and sustain their interest.

Many persons have contributed to this book in one way or another. Those I want to especially thank are:

Christine Conboy, Physical Education teacher, for her help with "Spring Into Fitness."

Dr. Robert McClure, Dermatologist, in Lilburn, Georgia, for his technical expertise on skin care and for his excellent care as our family dermatologist.

Anne Jackson, hairstylist, for her suggestions in finding the right hairstylist and added advice on hair care.

Russ Berkhan, owner of the Gentry Shop in Snellville, Georgia, for his consultation about the proper fit of clothes for men and his desire for people to look their best in what they wear.

Julie Daniel, owner of a lady's retail store, "For All Seasons" in Snellville, Georgia, who believes we are all special and have our own "fashion" personality. She believes we all need to find that "specialness" and enhance it.

Jane Mitchell, RN, for her thoughtful suggestions as to how to be a considerate hospital visitor and patient.

Edgar Brush, owner of Chick Filet at Peachtree Center in Atlanta, Georgia for his suggestions on employee excellence.

Tom Wuerslin, Delta Air Lines pilot and my husband and dear friend for over 22 years, for his comfort when I became weary from research and writing. Also, for his advice on air travel and the care of sports equipment.

Diann Veith, elementary school teacher, etiquette teacher, and dear friend, for her unfailing encouragement to write a book that would effectively communicate to the total young man and young woman and, especially, for her belief in me.

Diane Wuerslin, my precious daughter, for reading my manuscript as it came off the computer. Her accolades motivated me. As she and my sons, Paul and Mark, incorporated the lessons in this book into their lives I became even more determined to help other young adults through my book and classes.

Shannan Burnett, a very friendly preteen who read the initial chapters of my book to make sure I was writing with clarity for the young.

To my many, many students, for their eagerness in developing excellence in their personal and social lives and faithfulness in practicing their new skills.

And with great appreciation to. . .
Dr. Don Highlander Jr., Marriage and Family Therapist in Decatur, Georgia and author of "Parents Who Encourage, Children Who Succeed," without his guidance this book would not have been written. He cared about every word and expression to ensure positive and clear communication to young ladies and gentlemen.

INTRODUCTION

Dear Parent,

A short while after the death of his father, a seventeen year old boy drove his mother and sister to visit his father's brother. After fifteen hours behind the wheel, this young man happily pulled into his uncle's driveway. Almost as soon as their dinner was over, this young man disappeared. His only thought was to rest his body and find sleep. The boy's uncle became furious when he discovered his only nephew had gone to bed without saying goodnight. He stood outside his nephew's door and shouted, "I have the rudest nephew in the world. He can't even say goodnight to his uncle. I'll remember this." And remember he did.

The following morning, leaving his nephew behind, Uncle drove his niece to his clothing factory. You can imagine this little girl's delight when her uncle told her to select any five dresses she fancied. Uncle brought home an unfashionable tie for his nephew. This teenage boy would pay a price for the rest of his life for forgetting his manners. This true story took place twenty-five years ago, and Uncle has never forgiven his nephew for his thoughtless behavior.

We can learn from our mistakes and determine not to repeat them. God can also build compassion in us through our social errors. We can become more forgiving towards others when they exhibit poor manners. Unfortunately, some people only give you one chance. If you ever display behavior they find intolerable, they never forgive or forget -- no matter how hard you try or how much you improve.

Quest For Excellence targets fifth through eighth grade girls and boys. Most etiquette books stress learning skills that will encourage others to think well of them. This book doesn't teach personal and social skills to achieve social acceptance. Rather, this book emphasizes developing these skills to help gain self-confidence. As a young person acquires confidence, he/she becomes less conscious of self and more aware of others.

Making it possible for your preteens to like themselves and to know their purpose for living is both an art and an attitude. As you develop an attitude of confidence as parents, so will they learn confidence to reach out to others socially, emotionally, relationally and conversationally.

How will your preteens possibly take the time to read a book about personal and social skills? First, they will be drawn with you to the down-to-earth practical help illustrations throughout. Personal stories of teen struggles in overcoming embarrassing situations will motivate them to read these pages with anticipation. Learning to respect themselves and laugh at their mistakes will encourage them to get involved emotionally in these materials. They'll become less frustrated and less self-condemning. They will not see failure and self-consciousness as diseases, but rather as the key to learning and overcoming personal insecurities.

"Life Line" begins each chapter by giving spiritual application to the skills to be learned. Be sure to read the "More Helpful Hints" at the end of many of the chapters. Students enjoy these little jewels of information. Scattering this information throughout the chapters would maintain interest, as well. These helpful hints draw them into the book and get them hooked. Some of my students tell me they enjoy reading the stories and helpful hints before they read the material.

Families today, especially two-income families, have little time to teach their children proper social behavior and good grooming practices. This book can become a tool to help parents and children. Parents, for example, often nag at their children to pick up their rooms. They neglect to give concrete advice on how to better organize their rooms. My book helps solve this dilemma.

Parents of my students often tell me, "We have tried to teach our children to show kindness to others and to use proper table manners. They just thought we made up these rules until you taught them." My book is the authority parents need. Many parents cannot afford to enroll their children in a class such as I teach (in Christian and public schools, department stores, and private homes).

Parents read my book out of a desire to teach their children skills that will build their children's confidence. The "Dear Parent" letters at the end of the chapters give suggestions for helping your sons and daughters incorporate the rules and techniques in their daily lives. Peace and harmony become by-products in the family by working on these skills together. One student wrote to me, "After my mother and I organized my closet and drawers (as taught in my book), she and I worked together on her wardrobe."

Quest For Excellence fills the gap between little girls and senior high students. My book reaches out to the neglected male population, too. My book doesn't focus on manners alone. Young people learn excellence in personal grooming skills, exercise, interview and job skills. They also learn how to live in harmony with people they meet in everyday life. My book teaches balance. The young person learns not to focus on only one aspect of his life. Personal grooming skills and social skills complement one another.

Putting into practice the guidelines in this book will help the reader make the best use of the God-given talents we each possess and achieve his or her full potential. What more could a parent ask for their son or daughter?

Deborah Wuerslin
Don H. Highlander, Jr.

Contents

LIFE LINE
Implementing Excellence

Posture Performance

Man looks at the outward appearance, but the Lord looks at the heart.
1 Samuel 16:7 NIV

Because others do judge us by our outward appearance, it is important that we reflect what God has worked in our hearts.

Being an effective witness for Jesus Christ, is enhanced by having an attractive appearance. Young people who walk with confidence, are well-groomed, and wear clothes that complement their figure type attract others to them in a way that can create opportunities for communicating the good news to others.

Just as with school work, athletics and relationships, make a commitment towards excellence in your posture performance. Practice standing, walking and sitting properly at home, and good posture will become natural for you in public. When good posture becomes second nature to you, you will relax, focusing less on yourself and thinking more of others.

Good posture reflects a healthy mind, body and spirit.
-Deborah Wuerslin

POSTURE PERFORMANCE

"Hey, look at that cute boy walking down the hall. I bet he is athletic," commented Cindy. "He's probably a brain," sighed Sue. "Let's go meet him before every girl in the school discovers him."

Cindy and Sue glanced at the newest boy in school and quickly concluded that he was attractive, athletic, smart, and potentially popular. Whether these observations were true or not, this student radiated confidence. The way he walked down the hall gave these girls the impression he had it all together.

Your posture reflects part of the first impression people form about you. "Quest For Personal Excellence" begins, therefore, with "Posture Performance."

Everybody has a body language. Your facial expressions, the position of your body and how you sit and stand, tells people how you are feeling and what you think of yourself.

If you are tired from not getting enough sleep, exercise, or fresh air, your body will look limp, your head will droop down and shoulders will become rounded. When you are full of energy, you will stand tall and walk with sprint in your step and joy in your spirit. As a confident male or female, hold your head high, and wear a smile. Your posture will tell people you feel good about yourself.

Observe others' body language. Some people seem unapproachable because of a timid or fearful look. Others might appear judgmental because of a snobby look. Have you ever watched angry people? Their rigid bodies are not relaxed. Their clenched hands, narrowed eyes, and tightly pressed lips, all say "stay away from me".

Be aware of your own body language. When I am feeling shy in a room filled with people, I tend to look serious and aloof. Realizing this, I concentrate on smiling and making eye contact. Those around me feel more at ease and I usually forget my shyness. I'm happy and feel more accepted by communicating friendliness to others.

Having good posture makes you look friendly. When you keep your eyes on the ground and your hands in your pockets, you will not encourage friendships. People will have a difficult time getting to know you if you act shy, bored, or even snobby.

Research shows good posture is healthy. You breathe more easily because your internal organs are not pressed together as when you are in a slouched position. Better breathing makes you feel energetic.

Having a positive body language requires knowing something about posture. Even a person who does not have an expensive wardrobe or feels he or she hasn't good looking physical features, will look like a prince or princess by using good posture and expressing an interest in making others feel accepted.

Remember, others are self conscious, too. You can make yourself and others feel good about themselves by practicing good posture habits and techniques. Posture performance is the beginning of a happy social life.

LET'S TAKE IT FROM THE TOP!

Hold your head level. Pretend that a helium-filled balloon is attached to your head. Let the balloon pull you up straight, without your feet leaving the ground. If you tilt your head back, you will appear arrogant. If you look down at the floor, you might appear shy or have an uncaring attitude. Holding your head level allows you to make eye contact, express friendliness, and confidence.

> Head Exercise: Walk around the house with a small pillow on your head. The pillow will stay on if your head is level.

> Head Exercise: Head rolls are great tension relievers for your neck. Draw a large imaginary circle with your head. Look left, look up, look right, look down. Repeat several times before reversing direction.

15

Relax those shoulders. Stretch your shoulders back, lined up under your ears, neither rolled forward nor strained backwards. Shoulders tend to draw up when people are tense.

Shoulder Test: Lift your shoulders as high as you can and then drop them. The dropped position is the relaxed position. If I am feeling tense, I give myself this test to make sure that my shoulders are relaxed.

Shoulder Exercise: To relieve tension, roll both shoulders at the same time rotating them up, back, and down. Repeat this several times and then reverse, up, forward, and down.

When your shoulders are lined up under your ears, your chest will neither be sticking out nor caved in. Hang your arms naturally at your sides.

Arm Exercise: Besides the arm strengthening exercises described in "Spring Into Fitness", try shaking your arms and hands to release any tension. You will see runners shake out their arms before a race. Before I speak to an audience, I clench my fists and then relax them. This helps me to feel relaxed.

Hold your stomach in.

Stomach Exercise: Strengthen those abdominal muscles in an easy way. Think of times when you can concentrate on holding your stomach in as tight as you can (while still breathing!). Be creative. At every red light, I hold my stomach in until the light turns green. Perhaps you can tighten your tummy while brushing your teeth for two minutes.

Tuck your hips under so you are not swayback. Standing with your buttocks sticking out places a strain on your back and loses that long straight line.

Posture Exercise: Stand with your back against a wall or door with your feet together and about a foot away from the wall. Place one of your hands behind the small of your back. Now slide down the

16

wall to almost a sitting position. Press your back against your hand. Slowly slide back up the wall. If you do not feel continual pressure against your hand, you are tilting your hips back. Congratulations if you still feel pressure against your hand after you straighten up. Keeping your hips tucked, move away from the wall. Now you know how your body feels to have your hips in proper alignment. Hooray for you!

Relax those knees. Do not lock your knees.

Stand with your weight evenly distributed on both feet.

A high school friend of mine habitually stood with one leg stretched out to her side. One day, while talking to me, she tripped a classmate as he passed by. This poor young man was the new boy in class my friend yearned to meet. What an embarrassing introduction!

Good posture might seem impossible to you for now. You have so many things to think about. With daily practice, however, good posture will feel as natural to you as breathing.

STANDING TALL

Attention! Most people think that standing correctly means to stand stiff as a soldier. The chin held back does not allow for natural head movement. The shoulders are back so far that they feel pinned to a wall.

When you think of standing correctly, think up, not back. Do you remember that helium balloon pulling you up? Review each of the exercises in the good posture list to make sure everything is in place.

FOR BOYS ONLY********FOR BOYS ONLY*******FOR BOYS ONLY

POSTURE PERFORMANCE

STAND LIKE A MAN

The staggered stance is the natural way for you to stand when talking with your friends. Stand with your feet a few inches apart and your toes slightly turned out. Keep your feet lined up under your hips.

When delivering a speech or posing for a picture, stand with your feet together and your hands clasped in front of you or down to your sides.

PLEASE BE SEATED

Leaping and jumping on a chair or sofa causes dust to fly, damages furniture, stresses your back, and irritates your hostess. Rather than attacking a piece of furniture, approach a chair with dignity. Walk up to the chair and gently sit down. This step insures a safe landing and avoids missing the chair.

Slouching in a chair places stress on your back and reflects a sloppy appearance. A girl might judge you as being an insecure individual. An employer during a job interview will assume you are lazy. Someone else will consider you rude.

Attain a positive image by sitting up tall in a chair. You can sit upright and relaxed without looking rigid. A gentleman doesn't sit on his feet, Indian style. He may keep his feet flat on the floor next to the chair. He doesn't stretch his legs out in front, inviting someone to trip over them.

A gentleman may also sit with one foot flat on the floor and rest the side of his ankle of the other leg on his knee.

SMART MOVES

WALKING

Your friends often hear you walking down the hall before they see you. They can tell which friend is about to join their group by the sound of his walk. Some young men walk like elephants, pounding the pavement as

Present Yourself With Pride. Which is correct?

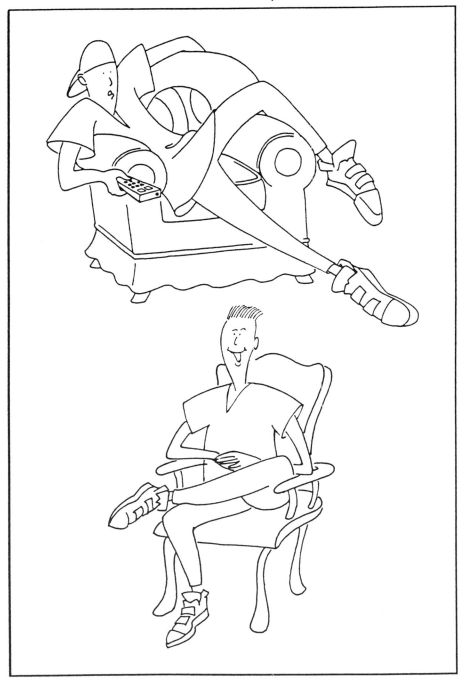

Successful Sitting

they walk. Others shuffle their feet, sliding and scraping their shoes down the hall.

Pounding hard on your heels is not only noisy but also jars your joints. Rather than walking flat-footed, roll off the balls of your feet and push off the toes. Your toes are pointed out slightly, not in as a penguin or way out as a duck. Neither your head, chest, nor hips, should lead the rest of your body. Maintain an upright posture, swinging your arms naturally at your sides.

One of my brothers took me Christmas shopping one year while I was in high school. I remember experiencing great difficulty in keeping up with my brother. His stride was much longer than mine. After huffing and puffing long enough, I asked him to stop. "Can't you slow down?" I asked. "I'm practically running to catch up with you." My considerate brother slowed his pace. He told me sometime later that he learned to walk more slowly with a date, because of our shopping adventure together. He discovered that females do not have as long a stride as gentlemen.

When you walk with a lady, accommodate your step and pace to hers. Slow down and enjoy her company. Offer to carry any package she may have.

STAIRS
Many young men enjoy flying up the stairs, taking them two at a time. Climbing stairs in this fashion will not impress a boss. Your date may experience difficulty keeping up with you. You may also end up slipping and sliding -- no way to keep your cool.

Climb stairs one at a time. Placing your entire foot on each step will prevent your foot from slipping and causing an embarrassing fall.

A gentleman guides a lady up and down stairs by gently holding her upper arm. I prefer for a gentleman to bend his arm at the elbow so I can slip my arm through his. Rather than pulling her, he walks next to her.

Escorting A Lady

When climbing a spiral staircase, a gentleman walks on the outside. Ascending or descending stairs on the inside of the spiral, allows a lady to take smaller steps. She does not have to worry about using the handrail because she has her arm slipped through the gentleman's arm. He will prevent her from falling in case she slips.

HELPING A LADY IN AND OUT OF A CAR

A lady enters the car first and exits last. A thoughtful young man walks around to the passenger side of the car and opens the door to help a lady in. He makes sure none of her clothing hangs out the door before gently closing it.

For exiting a car, a gentleman walks around to the passenger side of the car and opens the door for the lady. He may extend his hand to help her, especially if she has to step up onto a sidewalk or step down out of a truck or van.

Impress a young lady by driving safely. Keep both hands on the wheel and obey all traffic laws. She will respect you for thinking of her safety.

CARRYING A COAT

Dragging your coat behind you or wadding it up in a ball and stuffing it under your arm appears sloppy. Two ways of carrying your coat, projecting neatness, are: 1)Sling your coat over your shoulder, hooking your first two fingers under the collar or through the neck loop. 2)For a less casual look, carry your coat over your arm. Prevent your coat from dragging on the ground by folding it in half with the sleeves together. Tuck both sleeves under your coat as you put it over your arm. Now you won't have to bother with dangling sleeves. The open part of the coat faces you, giving you a neater look.

ASSISTING A LADY WITH HER COAT

Help your date, sister, mother, friend, or any female standing nearby. Ask before helping. "May I help you with your coat?" Face her back and hold her coat low enough so she does not have to reach up and high enough so it doesn't drag on the ground. After you help a lady out of her coat, carry it for

Always A Gentleman....

her, check it in a coat room, or fold it neatly and hand it back to her. In a restaurant or theatre, a lady may prefer to wear her coat to her chair. She simply sits down with her coat on. Assist her in pulling the sleeves off, draping the top part of the coat over the back of the chair.

CONCLUSION

Good posture reflects a positive attitude. Your positive appearance makes you appear friendly and trustworthy to others. Walking confidently into an office for an interview can make the difference in getting the job. Sitting correctly in class keeps you more alert, enabling you to perform better in school.

Assisting ladies portrays a thoughtful, caring gentleman. You make others happy and feel good about yourself when you display good manners.

Call this book your flight manual to living a successful life. Make "Quest For Personal Excellence" your checklist for beginning your journey towards excellence. Exercise, hair care, skin care, and dressing for success follow in subsequent chapters. Learn how to lift off through "Quest For Excellence" by discovering how to meet people, carry on conversations, entertain guests, and dine with confidence. Attain a smooth flight by becoming a thoughtful family member, neighbor, guest, shopper, traveler, and employee.

Every successful flight results from proper maintenance, a flight plan, and an alert, educated crew. These books teach you how to take proper care of yourself, how to become confident in your surroundings, and how to handle emergencies. You will become alert to the needs of others and build a reputation for your positive, caring way of living.

So, read on and enjoy your journey to "Quest For Excellence."

FOR GIRLS ONLY*******FOR GIRLS ONLY******FOR GIRLS ONLY

POSTURE PERFORMANCE

STANDING WITH POISE

You may stand with your feet together, but the preferred style is the clock stance. The front foot points to twelve o'clock and the back foot points to either two or ten o'clock. If the left foot, for example, is pointing to twelve o'clock, the right foot would be behind the left heel and pointing to facing two o'clock. Your arms can hang down evenly at your sides, or you can stagger them. If your right foot is back and turned out, your right arm can hang slightly behind you, really only a couple of inches behind your side.

The clock stance is a lovely way to pose for a picture. You will look poised and confident.

The staggered stance is a more natural way to stand when you are talking with your friends. Rather than standing in a clock stance or feet together, stand with your feet a few inches apart and your toes slightly turned out. Keeping your feet lined up under your hips.

WALKING WITH GRACE AND CONFIDENCE

Most individuals can be heard before they are seen. Each pounds her heels onto the floor and, single-handedly, sounds like a herd of elephants. Walking noisily is not walking gracefully. You want to give the appearance of gliding. Heavy walking also jars your body and can cause back and joint problems. Ask your mother or a good friend if you are a quiet or noisy walker.

The graceful walker appears to be gliding when she does not take the giant steps that throws her posture out of line. Instead she glides and takes small steps less than a foot-length apart (not baby steps, however). Her arms swing naturally from her shoulders rather than from her elbows as though she was running. Her toes point out slightly, not in as a penguin or way out as a duck. Forget the model who thinks walking on a straight line looks fashionable. She looks weird and not at all natural.

26

Timid Teen   Confident Beauty

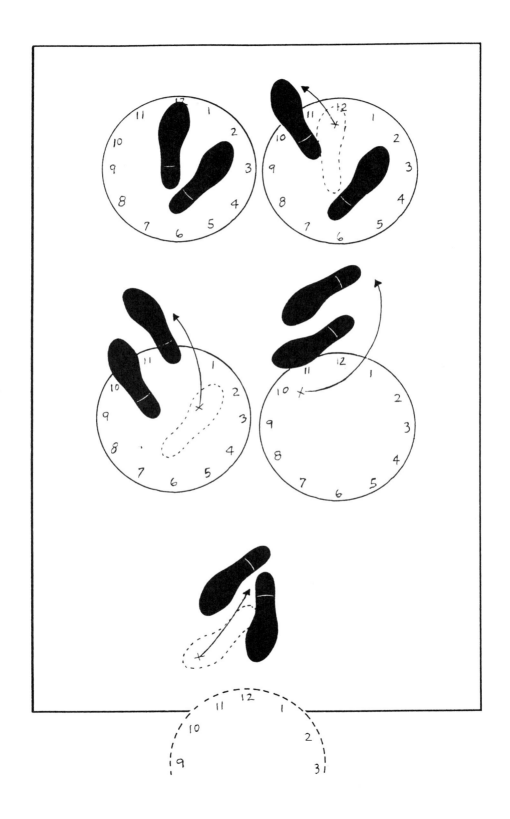

PIVOT TURN

Unlike a model's turn, executed with great flair, the pivot turn is a simple turn. When done correctly, you will look very natural and graceful.

All you have to remember is step, step, turn. When turning halfway around to the left, step out with the left foot slightly angled to the left. Then place your right foot parallel to your left foot, a few inches away. Now make a pivot turn. Lift up on your heels and turn on the balls of your feet. Finish in the clock stance with the left foot at twelve o'clock. Repeat step, step, turn to face forward again. When you want to turn right, step out to the right with your right foot. Finish your turn with your right foot at twelve o'clock and left foot behind the right at ten o'clock.

Practice this pivot turn so you can turn gracefully, without looking at your feet.

SITTING WITH POISE

Plop! Until taught correctly, people tend to collapse in a chair, and it takes several minutes for the dust to settle. This is unbecoming of a lady, hard on the furniture and jars the back.

Think of a chair as a delicate object, needing to be treated gently. Before you sit down, have the back of one leg touching the chair. If you try to touch the chair with both legs, you will have to bend over to sit down. Bending strains the back as well as losing that graceful motion. You are too far away if you cannot feel the chair with the back of your leg. How embarrassed you would be to miss the chair and find yourself on the floor!

As you slowly sit down, keep your head up, remembering that balloon again. You can now slide, not wiggle, to the back of the chair. If you cannot touch the floor with your feet, then the chair is too big for you. I suggest sitting on the edge of the chair.

What about those lovely legs and hands? How fun; you have several choices with both! Your feet can be flat on the floor, side by side, or in the clock stance position. When you cross your ankles, cross *under* and to one side. When your right foot is under, place your legs to the left and vice versa.

Slouch Queen

Sitting Pretty

Your hands can be placed in the center of your lap or to the opposite side of your legs. If your ankles are crossed and to the left, place your hands almost to the side of your right leg. Your hands look best either with fingers laced, or with one palm up and the top hand folded over it, facing down, palms together. You may also rest both hands facing down on your lap with one on top of the other.

Crossing your legs puts pressure on them and can give you unnecessary veins due to poor circulation. If you must cross, do not stick your upper leg out. Someone passing by could trip over it. Oh no, not again! Keep your crossed legs at a slight angle and close to your chair. Never dangle your shoe on your foot. Your shoes should always remain all the way on your feet when in public except at the pool or beach.

Are you ready to stand up? Uncross those ankles and slide to the edge of the chair. As you stand, keep your head up.

At first, you will look stiff, trying to sit down in a chair. With much practice, you will be able to be seated and rise again with the greatest of ease. Grace will have replaced plopping. How like a princess!

STOOPING

Stooping correctly is a wonderful way to strengthen your leg muscles. When executed incorrectly, by bending over at the waist, you strain your back.

Two rules to remember are: keep your body upright and your knees together. Approach the object you need to pick up at a slight angle, almost sideways. Stoop down, keeping your knees together and your head only slightly bent downwards. As you rise, keep your upper body upright. Use your leg muscles to help you.

Bend At Knees , Not At Waist

HANDLING STAIRS WITH GRACE

> Have you ever fallen going up a set of stairs? I have! Many years ago, my date and I were climbing some marble stairs to a theatre where we were to hear a concert. I felt so sophisticated in my lovely blue dress and matching heels. I did not pay attention to what I was doing, so I slipped and fell on the very top step. My backside pointed upwards for all the world to see. Embarrassed does not totally describe my feelings. I desperately wished for a hole to crawl into and hide.

Learning from my mistake, I received instruction on how to climb and descend stairs the sure-footed way. First, always pay attention to what you are doing. Becoming carried away with a conversation will distract you from climbing the stairs with grace. Secondly, glide your hand along the handrail rather than grabbing it. Thirdly, put your entire foot on the step so your foot does not have a chance to slip. Fourthly, step softly.

On your descent, continue gliding your hand along the railing. Face slightly towards the railing to help keep your balance. Also remember not to bounce. If you step softly, you will not have to worry about looking like a yo-yo.

PUTTING ON A COAT

Many young ladies put on their coats as though they were matadors in a bullring. They swing their coats to their sides and then fling them over their heads.

Here is a smooth way to put on your coat. You will look graceful and keep from messing up your hair. Hold your coat with your left hand at the top of the coat with your thumb facing up. Slide your right arm in the right sleeve. Take your right hand and grab the right lapel, letting go of the coat collar with the left hand. Now the left hand can reach behind and enter the empty sleeve. Lift your coat over both shoulders, making sure that the collar is out and flat.

To take off your coat, slip the left side off your shoulder. Reach behind you with the right hand and pull the left sleeve off your arm. Grab the

I'll fly away

Left thumb up, right arm in, hold coat with right hand on lapel, slide left arm in, adjust collar.

right lapel with your left and pull out of the right sleeve, being careful not to drag your coat on the ground.

CARRYING A COAT

When you carry a coat over your arm, do you find that it keeps coming partially off your arm and even dragging on the ground? You have to continually gather your coat and put it back over your arm. How frustrating and what a sloppy look.

Fold your coat in half with the sleeves together. Tuck both sleeves under your coat as you put it over your arm. Now you will not have to worry about dangling sleeves. The open part of the coat should face you, giving you a neater look.

GETTING IN AND OUT OF A CAR

Three good reasons to learn how to enter and exit a car correctly are: You will save your back from straining, you will look lovelier, and you will save someone from embarrassment from not having to look up your dress.

I'll make this simple. When entering a car, keep your knees together and lead with the knees. Tilt your head slightly so you do not hit it on the car, but remember to keep your posture upright. You can use your hands to push on the seat for extra help. When exiting, keep knees together, but this time lead with your feet.

CONCLUSION

Will they notice? No one will say, "Gee, you put on that coat correctly," or "I like the way you got into my car." What others will notice is that you are graceful and poised in everything you do. Your friends may not have good posture, and some of them may not want to. Without judging them, decide that you are going to be an individual. You will be a young woman of confidence   in everything you do, think, and say. You may not receive compliments by people your age, but they will admire you for having the courage to do what is best.

Knees And Toes Together

REVIEW
Posture Performance

1. What are two expressions of your body language? (Paragraph 4)
   a)
   b)

2. What are two reasons for having good posture (Paragraphs 8 & 9)
   a)
   b)

3. For good posture, hold your shoulders back as far as they will go. True or False?

4. Stand with your weight _____ _____ on both feet.

5. When standing correctly, think _____ not back.

6. The _____ _____ is a more natural way to stand. (Read under "Standing with Poise.")

7. Another way of standing is the _____ _____. ("Standing with Poise")

8. Before you sit down, what should you do?
   _____.

9. What should you always keep on in public, except for at the beach or pool?
   _____

10. When seated in a chair, what are two rules to remember before you stand up? (Read under "Sitting with Poise.")
    a)
    b)

Posture Performance

Dear Parent,

Read "Posture Performance" with your son or daughter. You will discover that good posture makes for a healthy, confident, and attractive person. Good posture means relaxed, natural, and friendly rather than stiff and snobby.

Good posture relates to how we move as well as how we sit and stand. Stooping to pick up an object, handling stairs with grace, putting on a coat, and getting in and out of a car are other opportunities for your son or daughter to practice grace and confidence in motion. The posture exercises will benefit every member of your family.

Remember to encourage rather than discourage. Teach rather than criticize. Your son or daughter will gain confidence more rapidly and be encouraged to practice these new skills.

Deborah Wuerslin

LIFE LINE
Implementing Excellence

Spring Into Fitness

I can do everything through him who gives me strength.
Philippians 4:13 NIV

Work daily to keep looking your best through exercise and fresh air, proper eating, adequate rest, and good grooming habits. Haven't you yet learned that your body is the home of the Holy Spirit God gave you, and that he lives within you? Your own body does not belong to you. For God has bought you with a great price. So use every part of your body to give glory back to God, because he owns it. 1 Corinthians 6:19,20 Living Bible

Some don't attempt to participate in a sport or an exercise program because they think they have to achieve status as star athletes. "Go for the gold," is the world's motto. It's all or nothing is often the attitude. But for others winning is making the effort.

> Olympic runner, Redmond, from Great Britian pulled a muscle in a race only half way around the track. Officials tried to help this injured runner, but he waved them away. His father came out of the stands and onto the track. He told his son, "We started this together and we're going to finish it together." Although the race was over, this Olympic runner leaned on his father. Together they slowly crossed the finish line.

Sometimes we try to establish our identity by what we do. However, achievement becomes status. Life comes from focusing on the spirit. We can get so caught up in athletics or exercise programs that we forget to be God directed. Redmond could have given up and emotionally died on the track. He chose life by leaning on his father. In your pursuit of physical fitness, lean on your heavenly father and be a part of mental, emotional, physical, and spiritual fitness.

"Give it your best shot," is God's desire for you. Set realistic and achievable goals. Attaining ace serves in every tennis game you play may be unrealistic.

After you set goals, set up a realistic schedule. Remember to incorporate cross training into your program. Put your plans into action! "The only place success comes before work is in the dictionary." Work hard and have fun.

In your "quest for excellence," remain a good sport and remember to encourage those around you. God will give you the strength to achieve your goals as well as the strength to face disappointments. Who you are in Him is much more important than merely what you achieve.

There are no riches above a sound body, and no joy above the joy of the heart.
"Runner's Day-By-Day Log and Calendar"

SPRING INTO FITNESS

"Exercise! That sounds like work to me."

"Sure, I know that exercise develops firm muscles and gives you good posture. Exercise also makes you feel better because you look more attractive and have increased energy. Breathing is easier and digestion is more efficient. But who wants to work so hard to keep in good physical condition?"

Many people cringe at the very word "exercise." They visualize themselves as sweaty and tired. They can almost feel their body racked with pain. They quit almost before they start.

Exercise can be fun. When you create a fitness program you enjoy, you will not experience boredom. You will find yourself anticipating your workouts. Exercise becomes enjoyable.

CROSS TRAINING

The key to a successful exercise program is cross training. When you alternate your activities, you will be more consistent. Most exercise programs fade away due to boredom, injuries, and lack of time. Through a cross training program, you attain greater strength, flexibility, and aerobic capacity by working your muscles and heart in various ways. To succeed, exercise has to become a part of life.

For busy days, exercise at home, cutting down on travel time. Jumping rope is good for all-over body improvement. This exercise is effective after fifteen minutes of steady jumping.

House and yard work can be an effective part of your cross-training program. Vacuuming, sweeping, gardening, painting, mowing the lawn, raking leaves, and shoveling snow provide exercise as well as giving you a sense of accomplishment. Now you can work through your chores with diligence, knowing you are building a stronger and healthier body.

Exercise at least three times a week for a minimum of 20 minutes of continuous movement. Choose an exercise program which includes exercises for flexibility, stamina, and strength building.

Stretching produces flexibility and can be done at home. Start stretching for five to fifteen minutes. Later, if you wish, you can increase your stretch workout time to thirty minutes. Stretching on a regular basis will keep you flexible and reduce injuries. Always execute these bending and twisting exercises before and after a workout. Hold each stretch for 30 seconds and never bounce.

Remember to warm up your muscles before stretching if you exercise early in the day. Warm-up exercises, such as a brisk walk or short jog, increase the blood and oxygen flow to the active muscles. Warm muscles will be more elastic and reduce stress from straining cold muscles.

A brisk walk is also an excellent cardiovascular exercise and helps keep your muscles from tightening up. Unlike running, you will not jar your joints. The fresh air, which benefits your health, is a bonus.

To build Stamina and a stronger heart and lungs, choose an aerobic activity. Through these activities, you use the body's large muscle groups in continuous, rhythmic, sustained movement and require oxygen for the production of energy. Some popular activities are aerobic dance, canoeing, cycling, cross-country skiing, jogging, roller skating, swimming, walking, and "wogging" (race walking).

Cut down on injuries by exerting different muscles with a variety of activities. Do not overwork any one muscle. A cross- training program, will improve your performance in a competitive sport, control your weight, and increase your strength and flexibility. You will also enjoy better health.

Strength-building exercises such as sit-ups, pushups and pull-ups can be executed at home. A good weight-training program will increase your strength and endurance. Your performance in sports will greatly increase by building stronger muscles.

> Jackie Joyner-Kersee won the gold medal in the 1988 Olympic Games in the long jump and heptathlon. Her cross-training made the difference. Jackie's weightlifting produced a stronger body for hurling the javelin and shot. Her strong arms enabled her to have a better pump to make her run faster. Her aerobic work gave Jackie endurance.

Breathe properly. Don't hold your breath during exercise. Muscles must have oxygen to move easily so breathe deeply, slowly, and rhythmically to reduce strain on your heart and hold off fatigue and sluggishness.

Cool down. Rather than ending a workout abruptly, a cool-down reduces the risk of injury to your skeletal muscles. Since muscles shorten and tighten during strenuous activities, you need to stretch them to relax them. Follow an aerobic activity with some gentle stretching and slow rhythmic movements for at least five minutes. Your cool-down may also be used as a warm-up before exercising.

SPORTS

Sports create an enjoyable atmosphere for acquiring exercise. When other people are involved, you also benefit from the fellowship.

A good way to make friends is to become involved in a sport. Below is a list of some sports that will help you to stay in shape as well as build relationships.

Aerobic Dance/Low-Impact Aerobics is a cardiovascular activity that improves blood circulation and breathing. Aerobics is good for overall exercise and helps with weight control.

Badminton, basketball and volleyball improve coordination. These sports improve coordination and strengthen your leg muscles and upper body.

Bowling is a fun social sport. Warm up and stretch before you play.

Cycling works the thigh, buttocks and lower back muscles without putting stress on your knees. Cycling tones your body and gives you a good cardiovascular workout. It is also an excellent time for meditation and reflection.

Dancing, such as square dancing and tap dancing, is another cardiovascular exercise. Ballet improves strength, balance and flexibility.

Frisbee Toss. Have you ever attended a serious frisbee "match?" Watch the participants leaping high into the air, stretching like rubber bands, and rolling like balls. A great deal of sprinting is involved. This new sport will teach you speed, balance, and help with flexibility.

Gymnastics, a good all-around sport, strengthens your heart, lungs and muscles. You develop defined muscles, flexibility and a keen sense of balance.

Hiking is a favorite exercise in my family. We enjoy the fresh air and scenery. What a fun way to strengthen your legs and get some cardiovascular exercise. As our endurance and confidence increases, we attempt more challenging trails.

Horseback riding strengthens posture and improves coordination.

Ice skating, Ice hockey, roller skating, and skateboarding are great arm and leg builders. These sports improve your balance, speed and stamina.

Racquetball improves coordination and increases endurance.

Rowing increases overall fitness, muscular endurance, and upper body strength.

Running, an excellent cardiovascular exercise, strengthens leg muscles and releases tension. Be kind to your feet, knees, and back; minimize running on hard surfaces.

Soccer and skiing work both the lower and upper half of the body. By strengthening your upper body, your performance will greatly improve. These sports develop a sense of balance, burn off calories, promote muscle endurance, stamina, and flexibility.

Swimming strengthens the entire body. You use all of your major muscle groups. Swimming is a complement to brisk walking and cycling because it strengthens the upper body and is one of the best cardiovascular exercises. Swimming aids blood circulation. Swimming does not stress your joints and muscles because there is no gravitational pull. I swim laps with an empty, plastic gallon milk jug in each hand. These "water weights" strengthen my arms and give me a harder workout without putting stress on my body. Many people today use hand paddles for water-resistance exercises. Swim laps or join water aerobics, a swim team, a water polo team, diving, water skiing, scuba diving, or synchronized swimming (water ballet).

Table tennis, a great social sport, improves coordination.

Tennis improves your endurance and agility and strengthens your arm and leg muscles. You need speed and muscular strength to perform well.

Water skiing enhances muscular strength and endurance and improves coordination.

Weight training strengthens and tones muscles by exerting muscles against resistance. Strength improves posture and is helpful in fat reduction and weight control. Everyday activities, such as running for the bus, picking up school books off the floor, or helping around the yard and house are easier when your muscles are well-toned.

At home, soup cans can substitute for hand weights to strengthen your arms and upper back. Your P.E. teacher or local sports store can give you weight-training exercises. Follow their instructions to prevent injuries.

FULLY EQUIPPED

Help prevent injuries and accidents. Choose proper equipment for your activities and sports. This is essential. Injuries discourage. Carefulness motivates and increases enjoyment.

Not all shoes are alike nor should they be. Shoes have come a long way since 1910 when Goodyear designed the first sneakers. Today's sport shoes are designed for different playing surfaces as well as the demands each sport places upon the body.

A sport shoe specialist can help you select the appropriate shoe for the sport you will be participating in. The salesperson will also consider the size and width of your foot, its shape, and how you walk. Do you walk on the outside of your feet or rotate in?

Wear shoes, which are designed for a particular sport, for that activity only. Wearing tennis or basketball shoes off the courts for daily use, for example, causes them to lose shock absorption quickly. The cleats on soccer shoes will wear down in no time if worn on surfaces other than the grass fields in which they were designed. Do not wear shoes designed for specific sports with street wear until you have retired them from that sport.

Once you have proper shoes, think of what other equipment you will need. Soccer players should wear shin guards while cyclists wear helmets. A snow skier will prevent snow blindness by wearing goggles. Cyclists often wear special gloves to absorb sweat and protect their hands.

Taking care of your sporting equipment will make it last longer and be safer to use.

A tennis racket left outside in the extreme cold or heat loses its effectiveness for play and can even be permanently damaged. Store your racket in a racket case indoors. Tape around the edges so the racket will not become nicked. Never throw your racket or slam it into the ground when frustrated with your performance, unless you're a pro and can afford many new rackets at the expense of negative attention. Rather than becoming angry, play harder with more accuracy. Self control, respect, and confidence go together. They are teammates.

Balls for basketball, football, soccer, and volleyball will play better and last longer if inflated properly. Keep a pump and inflation needle on hand.

The blades on ice and hockey skates will become dull or ruined when you walk on concrete without using blade covers. To prevent rust, coat the blades with silicone, especially when storing at the end of the season.

Bicycles require a great deal of care. Like any piece of mechanical equipment, keep the gears clean and free of dirt and grit. Keep the tires inflated properly. An under inflated tire wears out faster and makes it harder to pedal. The brakes should not be worn too far down. Tighten and adjust all bearings to prevent breakdown in the middle of a ride when you are far from home. Keep a cycling tool and tire repair kit with you.

The condition of your equipment will reflect your attitude towards exercise. Take good care of your equipment and it will become a friend, helping to keep you fit.

CLIMATE CONTROL

HOT WEATHER EXERCISING

During an outdoor exercise activity, heat and humidity can endanger your health. Many of us would never attempt to jog or golf in the midst of an electrical storm. We know that lightning can strike and kill. Yet, some people never give a thought to running or playing tennis when summer temperatures are soaring and the humidity is high.

Exercising in the heat can lead to heat cramps, heat exhaustion, and even a heat stroke. Dressing properly and exercising sensibly can prevent physical ailments due to the heat.

If you cannot exercise in the cooler part of the day, follow these guidelines.

- Drink plenty of water before, during, and up to several hours after exercising in the heat. Caffeinated drinks such as coffee, colas, and tea will dehydrate you. Water is best.
- Carry a high-energy snack for long workouts.
- Wear loose-fitting, light-colored clothes. Dark clothing will absorb the heat. Polypropylene and other synthetic fabrics draw moisture away from your body surface to keep it dry and cool. Perspiration becomes trapped under plastic or rubberized clothing and will not allow you to cool off.
- Apply sunblock before you begin to exercise. Use an alcohol-based sunscreen. Oils and lotions can block evaporation.
- Wear a visor or hat to keep the sun off your face and sunglasses to protect your eyes.
- A scarf tied around your neck filled with ice cubes feels "cool."
- Start off by exercising for short periods, no more than 20 minutes a day for the first week. Then slowly add 10 minutes a day.
- Pay attention to the humidity. It interferes with the body's natural cooling system -- sweat and evaporation. Even a 65-degree day with high humidity can be dangerous.
- Cool down slowly. Never drink an ice cold drink or head for the nearest air conditioned room. Failure to keep these important rules can be fatal!

COLD WEATHER EXERCISING

Hypothermia, a lowering of internal body temperature that can lead to mental and physical collapse, even death, is a danger to winter-sport enthusiasts. Hypothermia can result from exposure to extremely cold weather. Hypothermia can kill. Take this seriously. Many "expert" sportspersons have died of hypothermia.

Dressing properly and keeping dry, is the best defense against this condition. Clothing that keeps you warm at rest in the seventy degree weather keeps you warm on the run at five below.

- Apply sunblock before you exercise outdoors. Protect your lips and hands from becoming chapped. Wear lip protection and lotion or gloves on your hands.
- Wear several layers of lightweight clothing. The layers trap air, acting as insulation. Avoid cotton, which soaks up moisture and remains wet. Choose long underwear of polypropylene, a synthetic material that keeps sweat away from your skin. Wool or cotton sweaters or sweatshirts are best for the middle layer. Wear a water-resistant jacket and pants on top. Remove the top layers as you warm up.
- You lose a lot of body heat through your head. Wear a hat.
- Some prefer earmuffs for protection.
- Sunglasses protect your eyes.
- Jog in place indoors and stretch before exercising out in the cold to prevent muscle pulls, strains and cramps.
- Do not exercise in fog, rain, or snow where the visibility is poor. You increase your chances of running into objects or other unseen hazards.
- Carry a flashlight or wear reflective clothing at night.
- Drink water. For long workouts, carry a high-energy snack.

Don't be a fair-weather athlete. You can exercise in hot and cold weather if you dress sensibly and use common sense.

LISTEN TO YOUR BODY
Pain may be a warning to slow down.

Feeling chills, cramps, clamminess, or nausea during heat training is a sure sign of over exertion in the heat. Discontinue exercising, get out of the sun, and drink water.

Uncontrollable shivering, slurred speech, stumbling, or drowsiness are symptoms of hypothermia -- a condition of subnormal body temperature caused by exposure to cold.

IN SUMMARY

Enjoy a lifetime of physical activity. Prevent injuries. Dress sensibly. Exercise in moderation. Cross train. Take care of your body. There are no trade-ins.

MISCELLANEOUS EXERCISES

Little exercises here and there will make a big difference in the condition of your body. You don't have to wait for that big hour-long workout. You can benefit from miscellaneous exercises during your every day activities. Grab these bits of time to strengthen and stretch your body. Exercising is a way of life, not just a series of classes or a seasonal sport in which to participate.

I challenge you to find opportunities to exercise in between sports and regular exercise sessions. Squeezing a rubber ball while riding in the car will strengthen your grip. Stretching during a television program will help keep you flexible. Deep knee bends while brushing your teeth tones those leg muscles. Remember how I suggested that you suck in your stomach at every red light?

Be creative. Write these miscellaneous exercises down in your personal fitness book. List the activities with which you plan to combine them.

PLAN OF ATTACK

Remember, your goals in your fitness program include activities that produce flexibility, increase stamina, and build strong muscles. No longer think of a fitness routine as merely a set of floor exercises. Think balance.

A regular exercise program will firm up your flabby flesh and help you to reduce or maintain your weight. Your friends will tell you that you look more rested. You will tell them that you are sleeping better and have more energy. Studying is easier because you are thinking more clearly. Your consistent fitness routine helps you to be more resistant to infections, clear out the cobwebs, and reduce stress and tension.

I mentioned earlier that regular exercise strengthens your heart and increases blood circulation. Research now shows that, if you begin to exercise early in life, you will reduce or stop the changes of natural bone loss.

So get to work! Set up a fitness program and be faithful. Outline your fitness plan in a notebook. Incorporate miscellaneous little exercises into your daily schedule. Participate in a variety of activities and sports. Give yourself credit for any chores that help keep your body in shape.

Set short term goals. As you reach these goals, upgrade your fitness program, continuing to challenge yourself. Reward yourself periodically for your success.

Pace yourself and be sure to include a warm-up and cool-down period at each workout.

Good nutrition plays a major part on cardiovascular health and physical fitness. Your body will not function properly without a well-balanced diet. Talk with your parents, health teacher, or a physician about ways of improving your diet. Check out books at your local library on good nutrition and special diets for athletes.

Happy exercising! You are going to feel and look great!

MORE HELPFUL HINTS

♠ "Take rest as seriously as you take your training. Strength is developed not during the training phase but instead during the rest phase, when muscle tissue grows stronger."--Runner's World

♠ Keep your body relaxed when exercising. Make sure your stomach isn't distended; try to isolate the muscle you are working and really feel the effort there.

♠ Invite your friends over and make up some exercise routines together.

♠ Become involved in a sport. You do not have to be the best. You will benefit by making new friends and developing a healthier and stronger body.

♠ Lacing your shoes across rather than crisscrossed will reduce irritation of the endons on the top of your foot. Circulation is better for the toes.

♠ In hot weather, running through the spray from a hose may feel good, but it does not rehydrate you or decrease your body temperature much.

♠ During daylight hours, park your car far from the shopping mall and walk. Walk up or down the escalator instead of merely standing and riding.

REVIEW
Spring Into Fitness

1. A cross training program promotes fitness through a variety of exercises and activities giving you greater _____,
_____ and _____ by working your muscles and heart in various ways.

2. How often should you exercise each week and for how long?
_____

3. How can you make your body more flexible?
_____

4. An aerobic activity builds _____

5. Some strength-building exercises are _____,
_____, and _____.

6. Cooling down properly after exercise reduces the risk of
_____.

7. Playing basketball helps improve _____
and strengthens your _____ muscles and upper body.

8. What physical activity strengthens the entire body?
_____

9. Can a good pair of tennis shoes be worn for all types of sports and activities?   Yes or No

10. Drinking two big glasses of water before a sport or activity will keep you from becoming dehydrated. ("Hot Weather Exercising")   T or F

11. Wear a heavy jacket when exercising outdoors in cold weather. ("Cold Weather Exercising") True or False

12. Running through the spray from a hose in hot weather decreases your body temperature. ("More Helpful Hints")   True or False

Dear Parent,

Have you struggled with your son or daughter, trying to motivate him/her into getting some fresh air and exercise? Perhaps he did not like any of your suggestions as to how he should maintain a healthy body. Maybe she could only associate exercise with boring drills and lots of work.

"Spring Into Fitness" shows how building a strong, healthy body means fun, friends, and new experiences through cross training by participating in a variety of activities and sports.

Encourage your son or daughter to try new sports and group activities. Remind him that he does not have to become the star player but that dedication and fair play are most important. Teach your son or daughter the importance of using proper equipment, following the safety rules. His equipment will last longer when he learns proper care as well as proper storing when not in use.

Find some activities you and your son or daughter can participate in together. Hiking or tossing a ball back and forth are cost-free activities that afford time together for fresh air, exercise, and relationship building. Selecting a sport or activity that neither you nor your son or daughter has participated in before draws you closer together as you encourage one another.

Be an example by incorporating an exercise program into your own life. Let him see your determination to learn new skills with a positive attitude. Teach her how to cheer on her team without screaming negative comments at the opposition.

Spring into fitness and have fun together!

Deborah Wuerslin

LIFE LINE
Implementing Excellence

Hair Care

Don't copy the behavior and customs of this world, but be a new and different person with a fresh newness in all you do and think. Then you will learn from your own experience how his ways will really satisfy you.
Romans 12:1 Living Bible

Be beautiful inside, in your hearts, with lasting charm or a gentle and quiet spirit which is so precious to God.
1 Peter 3:4 Living Bible

Your hair is one of the first physical feature people notice about you. When you wear a hair style that complements your face shape and one which is easy to maintain, you can focus less on your appearance and concentrate on sharing God's love.

You are an individual. God made you unique. No one else was created exactly like you. Rather than following a hair style fad that may not fit your lifestyle or complement your face, find your own hair style. A hair stylist can assist you in finding a hair style that is both contemporary and complementary. Look through magazines, catalogs, and store brochures. Observe the styles. Get other's opinions. Research, observe, be aware, and make a conscious effort to constantly evaluate the styles and fads throughout your teen years.

As you improve your grooming habits, ask God to help you grow inwardly towards him. May your outward appearance become a reflection of a beautiful spirit, filled with love, joy peace, patience, kindness, goodness, faithfulness, gentleness and self-control.

FOR BOYS ONLY*********FOR BOYS ONLY*******FOR BOYS ONLY

You never get a second chance to make a first impression.
Will Rogers

PERSONAL CARE: HAIR

TOP-NOTCH HAIR CARE

Hair for animals provides warmth and protection. Whiskers, covered with many nerves, help animals feel their way through dark places. For humans, hair covers the head for cosmetic purposes.

Your hair can make or break you. A neat, conservative hairstyle pleases the eyes of many. Some people shy away from boys wearing outrageous hairstyles. You may be a fun and sincere person, but judged as a weird individual because of your hair.

Some employers judge messy, dirty hair as someone who might have lazy work habits. He also realizes that customers negatively judge his store by a messy looking employee. What a shame to miss out on a job opportunity because of shaggy, dirty, and uncombed hair.

Your hair is the first physical feature people notice about you. Make a positive impression by wearing a complementary, neat, and clean hairstyle.

FIRST-CLASS HAIRSTYLE

A good hairstyle can improve your looks. Find a barber or hairstylist who will help you find the right hair style for you. A good barber will make suggestions after studying your hair and face shape, as well as listen to your preferences. Take pictures to your appointment of males wearing hairstyles you like.

Keep your hairstyle simple. Spending 30 minutes styling your hair and using vast amounts of hairspray or gels makes your hairstyle an inconvenience. A simple haircut makes your life a lot easier, especially when you don't have a great deal of time to spend on your hair.

56

A good hairstyle can accent good features and hide bad ones. Take into consideration: the shape of your face, your jaw line, your forehead, and your ears. A long face needs fullness on the sides and less on the top. A large forehead looks better with some hair hanging over it. If you have large, protruding ears, you might want some hair to cover part of them.

A good hairstylist also considers whether your hair is thick or thin, curly or straight.

Choose a masculine hairstyle that complements your physical features and is easy to maintain. Consider your lifestyle. A swimmer, for example, might find a shorter hairstyle easier to keep up.

DRY SCALP

The scalp is the covering of the skull where your hair is manufactured and where the oil is produced. Some scalps are too dry. Did you know that dandruff can be caused by not brushing your hair, eating an improper diet, or using a shampoo with too much detergent? Use a shampoo loaded with oil, and massage well in your scalp and hair strands. A dry scalp needs moisture. Always use a conditioner after you shampoo. If medicated shampoos don't chase away those flakes, then see a dermatologist, a doctor who specializes in skin treatment.

OILY SCALP

Too much oil is produced, leaving hair greasy looking. Use water-based hair products, like gels, rather than shampoos and conditioners that contain oil. Balsam usually contains paraffin (wax) base to coat the hair. This will attract dust and dirt.

NORMAL SCALP

Lucky you, but very few.

THE BRUSH OFF

Heredity causes most baldness. Scalp infections and reactions to drugs or radiation can also bring about hair loss.

Maintaining a healthy head of hair requires simple upkeep through regular brushing, shampooing, and eating a balanced diet.

Brushing stimulates your scalp and lubricates your hair. For the gentleman with dry hair, brushing spreads the natural oils from the scalp all the way to the ends of the hair. Gently brush oily hair. Often oily hair still has dry ends and needs the oils brushed from the scalp.

Daily brushing stimulates the scalp to improve blood circulation. Brushing also removes surface dirt, untangles your hair, and helps control dandruff. Brushing before shampooing, catches the hair you have shed. Now it will not fall into the drain and clog it.

Your hair brush should have rounded ends or bristles with balls on the ends to prevent split ends and scratching your scalp.

For good hygiene, keep your hairbrush and comb clean. Soak them in the sink in a mild detergent or shampoo while you wash your hair. Use a fingernail brush to scrub your comb clean.

Don't borrow or loan out brushes or combs. Infectious diseases can be transmitted.

Gentlemen, keep a comb in your pocket, but don't try to be Joe Cool, combing your hair while walking down the halls. Combing your hair in public gives the impression you spend too much time thinking about yourself. Comb your hair in the bathroom, locker room, or at home -- and never at the dining table.

SHAMPOO TIME

Use a shampoo and conditioner specifically designed for your type of hair. Your shampoo tends to be more effective if you don't use the same one all the time. Use one brand one week and another the next.

Regularly shampoo your hair to keep bacteria from growing. How often you shampoo depends on your hair type. Oily hair needs to be shampooed more often than dry hair. An active person in sports, for example, might need to shampoo more often than someone who is not active.

Thoroughly wet your hair with warm (never hot) water. Pour a small amount of shampoo (about one tablespoon) into the palm of one hand and work up a lather using the other hand. Massage the shampoo into your scalp. Next, concentrate on working the shampoo into your hair to loosen the dirt. Do not forget to scrub well the areas above your forehead, around your ears, and your hairline on the back of your neck.

Rinse very well with cool water to open up your pores and to make your hair shine. Spend as much time rinsing as you did shampooing. Rinse well at the base of your neck, too. You only need to shampoo a second time if you hair is extra dirty. Too much shampoo on dry hair makes it dryer. Boys with dry or difficult to manage hair find using a shampoo with a conditioner effective and easy to use.

Towel dry your hair. Remember to hang up your towel when you are finished!

If possible, let your hair air dry at least fifteen minutes before blow drying. Never brush fragile wet hair. It is easily damaged and you could pull some of it out at the roots. A wide-toothed comb is acceptable to use on wet hair.

When using a blow dryer, hold it six inches from your hair, keeping it in constant motion.

Brush your hair thoroughly to help replenish the natural oils in your hair. Then style and brush your hair into place.

Although hairstyles change from time to time, regular haircuts, shampooing, and brushing remain constant. Hair maintenance becomes easy when you establish a regular hair routine.

FOR GIRLS ONLY*****FOR GIRLS ONLY*****FOR GIRLS ONLY

People are like stained glass windows; they sparkle and shine when the sun is out, but when the darkness sets in their beauty is revealed only if there is a light within.
Elizabeth Kubler-Ross

PERSONAL CARE: HAIR

Femininity usually brings to mind a gentle woman, sitting around looking pretty. The previous chapter has just dispelled this notion. Yes, ladies, you can be athletic and still retain your femininity. An important part of being a young woman of confidence of loveliness includes keeping your body in excellent condition through exercise and good nutrition. Good personal grooming reflects another aspect of being a young woman of confidence of loveliness.

The first physical feature someone usually notices about you is your hair. Your hair sets off your lovely face. Just as you wouldn't put a dirty, scratched, dull frame on a beautiful painting, you would not want your hair to be unattractive around your face. Make your hair the crowning glory to your face.

> My father was first attracted to my mother by admiring the back of her head. She was sitting a couple of rows ahead of my dad on a train. My father couldn't help admiring her long, thick, shiny and wavy, chestnut-brown hair. He could hardly wait for her to turn around so he could see if her face was as lovely as her hair! My father made a point of meeting my mother before the train pulled into the station. The rest is history.

HAIRSTYLE

Do you desire to look like someone else? Discover your own personal style. Create a hair style that does not draw undue attention to yourself. Keep your hairstyle simple, manageable and complimentary. Maintaining a hairstyle that looks good on you, will give you confidence. You will have less desire to copy others.

A good haircut enables you to wear your hair in different styles. My mother taught me long ago that no one will ever appreciate your best style if you always look the same. This thought comforted me on days when I thought my hair looked crummy.

The shape of your face is an important consideration. Most people do not have that perfect round, oval, square, heart, or diamond-shaped face. Just remember to keep your hair in balance with the shape of your face. If you have a full face, the fullness on the sides would make your face fuller. The balance would be height on top and length on the sides. If your face is long, bangs will give it a shorter look. Wearing a hairstyle with fullness on the sides would help to round out your long face.

Besides lifestyle and face shape, your forehead, cheekbones, eye size and the texture of your hair are other factors to consider when deciding the right hairstyle for you. Your hairstyle, therefore, cannot be determined by a set formula. Your hairstyle must be designed specifically for you. Doesn't that make you feel special?

Just as you attempt to "dress for the occasion," style your hairdo appropriately for your activity. Wearing a glamorous hairdo playing basketball or on a camping trip would look out of place. If you only feel comfortable in a casual hairstyle, then for special occasions, add a jeweled comb, bow, or special barrette to your hair.

One of the best favors you can do for yourself is to find a hairstylist you can trust. A professional can keep you up-to-date on current styles. She can give you a personalized hair style and hair care tips.

Guidelines to finding the best stylist for you:
- Stop by and check out the salon. The appearance of the salon tells you how the owner feels about her business.
- Talk to the receptionist about services offered and prices.
- On your first appointment, a good stylist will observe how your dry hair falls and curls.
- The stylist will examine your facial features.
- A good hairstylist asks about your lifestyle in order to decide how to style your hair. Do you only have a few minutes in the morning to fix your hair? Do you spend a lot of time swimming? Are you a

ballet dancer who needs longer hair? Do you use electric rollers or a blow dryer?

- A stylist will ask your likes and dislikes as well as which hairstyles have not worked for you in the past. Looking through style books together helps the stylist to determine your taste. The stylist will also be able to show you styles best suited for your hair, face, and lifestyle. Be wary of the hairstylist who makes no suggestions.

- A hairstylist makes sure you understand every service you will receive as well as the price.

- A skillful stylist cuts your hair in a definite pattern instead of darting all over your head.

- The helpful stylist tells you how to style and maintain your own hair and which products to use.

- A good stylist listens to you when you politely mention you do not care for the cut or style you received at your last appointment.

- A stylist makes periodic suggestions for updating your hairstyle.

Visit your hairstylist about every six weeks, depending on your hair growth rate. Make an appointment before your hair looks shaggy or becomes damaged. Trim split ends or they will break off.

Never tell your hairstylist, "Surprise me." You may be sorry you did not express yourself. You and your hairstylist need to work as a team.

HAIR CARE

Learning ways you can abuse your hair is part of learning how to care for your hair. Constant use of curling irons, electric rollers, pulling your hair when you blow dry, rubber bands, and sun exposure without a conditioner can cause your hair to be dry and brittle. Not washing oily hair often enough will give you a greasy, dull look.

DRY SCALP

Your scalp is both where your hair is manufactured and where the oil is produced. Some scalps are too dry.

Normal scalps shed dead cells, causing little flakes of dead skin to appear on the scalp. Persistent and severe flaking is called dandruff. Dandruff can be caused by not brushing your hair, eating an improper diet, sleeping in curlers, excessive central heating, or using a shampoo with too much detergent. Use a shampoo loaded with oil and massage well into your scalp and hair strands. A dry scalp needs moisture. Always use a conditioner after you shampoo. If medicated shampoos don't chase away those flakes, then see a dermatologist, a doctor who specializes in skin treatment.

OILY SCALP

Too much oil is produced, leaving hair greasy looking. Use water-based hair products, like gels, rather than shampoos and conditioners that contain oil. Balsam usually contains paraffin (wax) base to coat the hair. This will attract dust and dirt.

NORMAL SCALP

Lucky you, but very few. Still use a conditioner. Talk with your hairdresser.

THE BRUSHOFF

Which brushes are best for you?

Fine Hair - Use a soft-bristle brush such as a natural bristle brush.

Medium Hair - Natural or synthetic bristle.

Coarse Hair - Very stiff bristle.

Your hair brush should have rounded ends or bristles with balls on the ends (except for the natural bristle brush). The rubber-based, plastic bristles brush grasps hair more easily, helping to prevent split ends.

Brushes are round, half-round, oval and rectangular. Your hair length, style, and brushing technique will determine the shape of your brush.

Brushing stimulates your scalp and lubricates your hair. For the young lady with dry hair, brushing will spread the natural oils from the scalp all the way to the ends of the hair. Oily hair should be brushed gently. Often oily hair still has dry ends and needs the oils brushed from the scalp.

To brush, bend forward at the waist with head down. Start at the ends of your hair and gradually work your way up to your scalp. Start with short strokes and gradually use longer ones. You can use your fingers of your empty hand to help free the tangles. Brush that scalp!

Brush your hair before you shampoo. You will remove any surface dirt as well as untangle your hair. Your parents will be grateful, too. Brushing before shampooing catches the hair you have shed. Now it will not fall into the drain and clog it.

Don't borrow or loan out brushes or combs. Infectious diseases can be transmitted.

SHAMPOO TIME

Use a shampoo and conditioner specifically designed for your type of hair. Your shampoo tends to be more effective if you don't use the same one all of the time. I use one brand one week and another the next.

Shampoo your hair regularly to keep bacteria from growing. How often you shampoo depends on your hair type. Oily hair needs to be shampooed more often than dry hair. Your lifestyle plays an important factor, also. A person active in sports, for example, might need to shampoo more often than someone who is not active.

Treat your hair gently to prevent tangles and breakage. Thoroughly wet your hair with warm (never hot) water. Pour a small amount of shampoo (about one tablespoon) into the palm of one hand and work up a lather using the other hand. Massage the shampoo into your scalp, using your knuckles. If you use your nails, you will scratch your scalp and also ruin your lovely manicure. Next concentrate on working the shampoo into your hair to loosen the dirt. Do not forget to scrub well the areas above your forehead, around your ears, and your hairline on the back of your neck.

Thoroughly rinse your hair. Spend as much time rinsing as you did shampooing. Rinse well at the base of your neck, too. Rinsing with cool water will close the cuticle in your hair and make your hair shinier.

You only need to shampoo a second time if your hair is extra dirty. Too much shampoo on dry hair will make it dryer. Two excellent rinses to remove shampoo buildup are: 1)Half cup of vinegar to one quart of water, or 2)Baking soda mixed with water. These will also help cut scalp and hair odor.

Apply a conditioner for your hair type (dry, oily or normal). If your hair is long and your scalp oily, condition only the ends of your hair. Follow the label directions. Finish your shower while your conditioner is working for you. Rinse well. Always keep your eyes closed to keep out the shampoo and conditioner, but do not squint. Squinting causes unnecessary wrinkles.

Squeeze out excess water with your hands, then towel dry your hair. *Never* rub. Rubbing will give you split ends. Instead, squeeze your hair with your towel or wrap the towel, turban style, on your head.

If possible, let your hair air dry at least fifteen minutes before blow drying. Never brush fragile wet hair. It is easily damaged and you could pull some of it out at the roots. Brushing wet hair will also stretch out your hair to its fullest, causing it to lose its elasticity. You could pull out your perm. A wide-toothed comb is acceptable to use on wet hair. Start gently combing at the ends and work up to the scalp, never tugging at your hair.

Before blow-drying your hair, apply a conditioning lotion or mousse gel. It will protect your hair from heat damage and add volume and shine. Hold your blow-dryer six inches from your hair and keep it in constant motion, no more than 5 seconds in one spot. Too much heat robs hair of precious moisture causing dry and brittle hair. To add volume, start drying at the roots. Your hair must be almost dry before styling and completely dry before using a curling iron.

Hair maintenance might sound like too much work. Once you establish a regular hair routine, as with your skin and nail care, you will find daily upkeep easy. Commitment and dedication are first steps to taking care of your hair.

MORE HELPFUL HINTS

♠   Use a spray-on moisturizer to condition hair. Apply while your hair is still damp and warm from shampooing.

♠ Use scarves, decorative hair combs, flowers, covered rubber bands, barrettes, flowers, ribbons, and hats for hair accessories.

♠ You do not need to hide behind your bangs; keep them trimmed to the middle of your eyebrows.

♠ Fabric softener in your towel can give you limp hair.

♠ For hair shine: Squeeze fresh lemon juice on your hair when you rinse it.

♠ Keep your blow-dryer in top shape by cleaning hair and lint out of the vents. Unplug the dryer first and use tweezers to pull out the hair and lint.

♠ Calm down frizzies after blow-drying by adding a small amount of gel or mouse to your hair.

♠ Instead of applying mousse or gel with your hands, put some on your comb or brush. You'll get more even distribution (no clumping) in addition to holding your hair exactly where you want it.

REVIEW
Hair Care

1. If you trust your hairstylist, should you tell him/her to "surprise you" the next time you want a hair cut? ("Hairstyle") Yes or No

2. What factors should you consider when deciding on a hairstyle?

       a)
       b)
       c)

3. Does it matter what type of hair brush you use? Explain.

_____

4. Shampoo your hair regularly to keep _____ from growing.

5. Besides washing your hair, your _____ needs cleansing and massaging, too.

6. Calm down frizzies by adding a small amount of _____ or _____ before or after blow drying your hair. ("More Helpful Hints")

Dear Parent,

Trying to follow the latest hair trend often leads to frustration. Your son or daughter may not have hair that lends itself to current styles. The right stylist, however, can adapt a popular style to his or her particular hair, face shape, and activities. Select a hairstylist, following the guidelines in this chapter, who will work with you and your son or daughter.

"Hair Care" shares valuable information on hair treatment along with the use of proper equipment. Your son or daughter will also enjoy the "tricks of the trade" shared throughout.

A hair maintenance routine can become as automatic as brushing teeth and promote healthy and attractive hair. With the right hairstyle and proper care, your son's or daughter's hair will become his/her "crown of glory."

Deborah Wuerslin

LIFE LINE
Implementing Excellence

Skin Care

But we Christians have no veil over our faces; we can be mirrors that brightly reflect the glory of the Lord. And as the Spirit of the Lord works within us, we become more and more like him.
2 Corinithians 3:18 Living Bible

No magical spell is going to transform you from an average looking young lady or gentlemen into one of confidence. You will need to work to attain poise. Practice makes poise and etiquette a natural part of your life. Work daily to keep looking your best through proper eating, exercise and fresh air, adequate rest, and good grooming habits. Learning how to take care of your skin and hands is important for good health as well as having an attractive appearance.

Is there anything more important than a flawless complexion? Yes! Those who radiate from their inner beauty. They have learned to let love, kindness, and joy that Jesus has put in their hearts to shine for others to see.

"You are what you eat." What a big responsibility God has given us to take care of our bodies. Eating a balanced diet *does* make a difference in your health and body growth. Eating junk can also affect your disposition as well as your skin. Feeding your soul is just as important as proper exercise and diet. *The good man brings good things out of the good stored up in his heart...for out of the overflow of his heart his mouth speaks.* Luke 6:45 NIV.

How do we make our heart more like our Lord's? We grow closer to Him through daily prayer, reading God's Word, and fellowshipping with other Christians. A balanced spiritual diet and food selection are both related to being an effective healthy person.

The way to gain a good reputation is to endeavor to be what you desire to appear.
Unknown

SKIN CARE

Skin, your largest organ, protects your body in many ways. Taking special care of your skin is the foundation of your beauty treatment. Wearing the best-looking clothes will not hide skin that has been abused, unless you plan on covering yourself from head to toe.

Have you ever noticed the softness of a baby's skin? Unfortunately, a person's skin is exposed to dust and dirt in the air, changing temperatures, the wind, the sun and water, harmful chemicals, and jolts and bumps. These elements can harm your skin. Pollution in the air clogs pores, causing blackheads and pimples. Sun exposure triggers wrinkles. Repeated exposure to the sun can lead to skin cancer.

Your skin can look radiant with proper skin care, making you feel and look your best. Learn to take care of your skin now and it will be in condition to handle the aging process.

SKIN TYPES

Dry: Flaky with occasional patchy red areas and a dull appearance; wrinkles easily. Wash only once or twice a day. Use a moisturizer.

Oily: Shiny, large pores, occasional blackheads and pimples. May be sensitive and susceptible to allergies. Oily skin tends to develop wrinkles less easily. Wash at least three times a day with a medicated soap. Use an astringent regularly.

Combination: Areas in the "T" zone (forehead, nose, mouth and chin) are oily. Areas around the eyes and cheeks are dry. Most of us have this combination skin. Wash in the morning and at night. Use a moisturizer on the dry areas and an astringent on the oily areas.

Sensitive: Skin is easily irritated by extremes in temperature, cosmetics, and some detergents. This skin type, the most prone to allergies, is characterized by dryness. Wash morning and night with a hypo-allergenic soap or cleanser. Also use products that contain no fragrance. Your face will be easier to keep clean if you keep your hands off of your face.

SKIN AND DIET

"You are what you eat." What a big responsibility you have to take care of your body!

Eating a balanced diet *does* make a difference in your health and body growth. You need to eat nutritious food for muscular activity when you work and play. Healthy food produces fuel necessary to heat your body and enables your body to work efficiently. Eating correctly also gives you the proper nutrients needed for continual body repair and maintenance of all tissues.

The basic nutrients in food are vitamins, minerals, protein, fats, carbohydrates and water.

Think fresh. Fresh fruits and vegetables as well as lean meats, fish, poultry and whole grains play an important role. Eating junk foods can affect your disposition as well as rob you of vitamins.

Some great snack foods are: nuts, raw carrots and celery, fresh fruit and popcorn.

To help keep your complexion clear, drink eight glasses of water a day (colas and tea do not count.). Water aids circulation and carries nutrients to all parts of the body. Water also regulates body temperature and cleanses the body of waste materials. An orange, lemon, or lime slice gives a refreshing taste to a glass of iced water.

SKIN AND FRESH AIR AND EXERCISE

Do you sit in class all day and then go home and plop in front of the television? Exercise is a must for keeping your body in tone, skin healthy and the cobwebs cleared out of your mind. Ever feel uptight? Try taking a brisk walk around the block. Remember to incorporate some form of exercise in your daily routine.

SKIN AND SLEEP

When you sleep, all of your activity decreases and your muscles relax. Sleep restores energy to your body. You should get 9-12 hours of sleep a night. Adequate rest will enable you to wake up with a smile on your face and your skin looking healthier. Gone will be those dark circles or bags under your eyes from staying up too late.

SKIN PROTECTION

You have probably been hearing a lot of talk about our ozone layer wearing away. The thinner this protective layer in our atmosphere becomes, the more damage the sun can do to your skin.

Wear sunblock daily. Apply 30 minutes before you go outside. This will give the sunblock a chance to adhere to your skin before you go outside and sweat it off. If your skin is oily, wear an oil-free sunblock.

Alex Znaiden, Avon's director of skin care research and development says, "Research shows if a sunscreen with a sun protection factor (SPF) of 15 is used from ages one to 18, over 75% of skin cancer can be prevented."

Most of us forget about our hands. Use sun block there, too.

Sun glasses will protect your eyes and cut down on wrinkles around the eyes -- "crow's feet."

Your lips need protection. You can use a lip balm, sunblock stick, or a lip moisturizer. Dry, cracked and flaky lips are neither attractive nor healthy.

SKIN AND SWIMMING

Always rinse salt water and chlorine off of your skin after swimming. Reapply sun block if you stay outdoors and apply lotion if you go indoors. Your skin will say, "Thank you for the drink (of moisture)."

A Glove For Every Occasion

GLOVES FOR PROTECTION

Gloves were originally designed to protect hands from cold weather and rough work. Later, they were made to wear as an accessory to an outfit, a decoration.

Your wardrobe should include a variety of gloves for different jobs and functions. Protect your hands and you will prevent them from becoming injured on a job. Wear gloves in cold weather, and your hands will not become dry and cracked.

- Rubber gloves for washing dishes, cleaning floors and bathroom
- Gloves for yard work
- Sports glove
- Gloves for cold weather
- The invisible glove -- sunblock with moisturizer for outdoor activities

LET'S FACE IT!

What does your face reveal?

Your face will reveal your inner self. Does your mouth frown or radiate a friendly smile, showing love and kindness towards others? Do your eyes squint in anger or impatience or are they pleasant, showing friendliness and peace? Does your face look tight and snobby or relaxed and gentle? Have you ever known anyone with good-looking facial features but an unkind heart? Was he or she really attractive to look at?

As mentioned earlier, your face will also disclose your sleeping habits, diet, exercise, and skin care. By taking care of your skin, your face will be attractive for others to admire. Your face will reflect the message, "I like myself enough to take care of myself."

FACIAL IMAGE

A clean face comes first.

Give your face the mirror check. Is your face reflecting good health and confidence?

Your Face Is An Emotional Mirror

Nothing can ruin a stunning smile more than unattractive teeth. Keep that smile bright by brushing your teeth, tongue, and gums 2-3 times a day, along with daily flossing and dental checkups twice a year.

Braces are in! Do not cover that smile. Let it shine. Tell your friends your smile is proof of your sparkling personality.

Never remove your retainer in front of others. Store it in a case when not in use to keep it clean and from danger of breaking.

Gum chewing is out! No lady or gentleman chews gum without looking like a cow chewing its cud.

Buy your eyeglasses from a professional who knows how to fit you properly. He will also make sure they complement your face shape and size.

For a neat appearance, keep your glasses sparkling clean. Your vision will not be impaired and others will be able to see your attractive, smiling eyes.

Wear sunglasses to avoid squint lines. Skin around your eyes is the thinnest, so squinting easily compresses the skin and gives you crow's feet. Sunglasses also protect against wind and pollution.

The information that follows will teach you how to properly care for your skin. As you establish a regular personal grooming routine, continue to reflect kindness and consideration towards others so that your outward and inward self may be one.

FOR BOYS ONLY*******FOR BOYS ONLY********FOR BOYS ONLY

May the outward and inward be one.
Socrates

PERSONAL CARE: SKIN

FACIAL GROOMING

Gentlemen, your face has the power to draw people to you or make them turn and run. A clean, healthy-looking face that beams with happiness and confidence encourages social relationships.

Just as you maintain a neatly-combed, trimmed hairstyle, establish a daily skin care program through proper cleansing, eating, sleeping, fresh air, and exercise.

Wash your face in the morning and at night and after a physical workout to remove dirt and dead cells.

- Wash your hands.
- Use a soap designed for your skin type.
- With soap, work up a sudsy lather in your hands, first.
- Apply soap gently to your face and neck, using upward and outward strokes. Wash gently. Harsh rubbing can irritate your skin and damage the fragile area around your eyes.
- Rinse with warm water.
- Splash cool water on your face to close your pores.

Washing your face includes cleaning the matter in the corner of your eyes and the dirt in and around your ears and on your neck.

AN AWARD-WINNING SMILE

Nothing like a brilliant smile to light up someone's life! Brushing your teeth after every meal prevents tooth decay and unsightly yellowing due to plaque build up. Flossing daily removes food particles between your teeth and helps prevent gum disease.

SHAVING TIPS

When the time comes, you will want to know how to shave smoothly, without cutting yourself. You won't have to wait until you can grow a mustache or beard. Even "peach fuzz" under your lip and on your chin appears sloppy and should be shaved.

THE CUTTING EDGE

Determine which type of razor you want to shave your face.

1) Electric razors, little hand-held machines powered with motors. They run on electricity or batteries. The head of this razor passes over the skin and clips the hairs. Electric razors are more effective with cutting hair that stands straight rather than hair that curves or lies at a slant.

The head on an electric razor needs replacing or sharpening when it becomes dull.

2) Safety razors are metal or plastic holders, containing sharp blades. When the blade (or twin blades) becomes dull, it is removed, thrown away, and replaced with a new blade.

3) Straight-edged razors look like a long knife attached to a handle. Mostly used by barbers, these razors must be sharpened regularly.

For a close shave, use a safety or straight-edged razor, especially if your hair curves or lies at a slant. Some men shave against the lay of their whiskers to get a closer shave. This technique, however, can cause skin irritation or "ingrown hair".

Using hot water, lather the part of your face to be shaved with shaving cream. The cream softens your whiskers, making them easier to cut and provides lubrication for the blade so it doesn't cut you.

Use only sharp blades for shaving. Dull blades cause nicks and cuts.

If you cut yourself, dip the end of a styptic pencil in water and gently rub it on the wound. This application may sting but will stop the bleeding. Another popular technique is to place a small section of tissue over the cut area. The drawback to this method is that the bleeding may start again when you peel off the dried tissue.

While you are shaving, trim any hairs that are hanging out of your nose. Be careful when using even small scissors near your face.

Aftershave or cologne smells great when used sparingly. Someone smelling your "scent" across the room means you have too much of a good thing.

SKIN AND CLEANLINESS
In countries where people do not bathe, they smell badly. Unclean people also have problems with disease and epidemics -- disease that spreads rapidly to many others and is out of control.

Although soaking in the tub may relieve sore, tired muscles, a shower removes dirt more easily and quickly. Shower daily and more often after physical workouts or when necessary. You don't want someone to smell you before they see you.

Gather all of your supplies before you turn on the water: soap, a towel and washcloth, nail brush, back brush, shampoo, clean clothes or pajamas.

Before showering, trim your finger and toe nails. Soft nails after showering are difficult to cut.

Soak your hairbrush and comb in a mild detergent while showering.

After showering, gently push back your finger and toe cuticles with the end of your towel. Dry off vigorously to promote blood circulation. If your skin is dry, just pat your skin dry and apply lotion.

Unless you are going to bed, apply deodorant.

Leave the bathroom in perfect order. Polish the chrome shower fixtures dry and remove any hair on the floor of the shower. Hang up your towel and wash cloth and put your dirty clothes in the hamper or laundry room. Your mother will appreciate your thoughtfulness.

NAIL CARE

A proper diet helps keep your nails healthy. Detergents, chlorine in pools and weather can cause them to be soft and brittle. Nails are very porous so they absorb water. When they dry out, they lose the water and split or peel. Keep hands dry by wearing gloves. You can also apply a moisturizer or oil on them.

Yes, gentlemen can use moisturizers and lotions. Rough, cracked hands and splitting nails are not attractive. Use a non-scented moisturizer, especially after you shower. For very dry hands, arms, and legs, apply Crisco, a pure vegetable fat, to your damp skin. Rub in well, so as not to stain clothing. The results will be pleasing to the eye and the touch.

Gently push back cuticles with the end of a towel after showering.

Short nails are easier to keep clean and appear more attractive. Keep a nail brush on hand to scrub the dirt from under your nails. For good personal hygiene, wash your hands whenever you use the bathroom, when you arrive home from public places (including school), after chores, and before handling food.

Use your manicured, clean hands to reach out to others. Help with chores around the house. Greet a newcomer with a friendly handshake. Carry a package or books for a lady. Wave hello to a passing neighbor. Practice those tennis or basketball shots with determination and good sportsmanship. Work diligently on a job.

Prevent your hands from destroying your body through the use of drugs. Keep your hands away from literature unbecoming of a gentleman. Refuse to use your hands to damage someone's property.

Employ your hands in positive activities.

YOUR FEET

Treating your feet with kindness guarantees comfort and good health. Keep your toenails clipped. Long nails will rub against your shoe, causing your toes to hurt. Long nails split and break off. Clip your toe nails straight across to avoid ingrown toenails. Give them a smooth edge by filing them with an emery board.

SHOES -- A PERFECT FIT

- Buy shoes for comfort or your feet will be screaming at you by the end of the day.
- Shop for shoes in the late afternoon when your feet are somewhat swollen.
- Fit the larger foot.
- Make sure the shoe fits the widest part of your foot. Don't count on it to stretch to fit.
- Give your big toe 1/4" - 1/2" space to move.
- Wear socks with your shoes.

KEEPING FEET FIT

Exercise your feet by rolling them back and forth over a can. Walk around on the balls of your feet. During your shower, stretch up on the balls of your feet and then relax. Repeat several times. You can do this while you brush your teeth, as well. I love to combine exercise with another activity.

Take care of your skin and you will look and feel great.

FOR GIRLS ONLY*******FOR GIRLS ONLY******FOR GIRLS ONLY

There is no cosmetic beauty like happiness.
Unknown

PERSONAL CARE: SKIN

SKIN AND CLEANLINESS
In countries where people do not bathe, they smell badly. Unclean people also have problems with disease and epidemics -- disease that spreads rapidly to many others and is out of control.

Since ancient times, people have enjoyed bubble baths, natural-hot baths, salt-water baths, and oil baths. Although a daily shower cleans your skin better, an occasional beauty bath is very relaxing.

I like to take a beauty bath after a long, busy day to help relieve tension. I gather everything I need while my bubble bath is filling up. Here is what you need:

- Bubble bath or baby oil
- Nail clippers or scissors
- Headband
- Towel and washcloth
- Soap - use soap for your skin type
- Back brush
- Nail brush
- Manicure stick
- Razor
- Loofa sponge or pumice stone
- Powder
- Perfume
- Clean clothes or pajamas

Before bathing, trim your toe nails. Smooth edges with an emery board. Pull your hair back in a pony tail or use a headband. Soaking in the tub gives you the opportunity to put a cleansing masque on your clean face. Soak in the water for 15 minutes. Relax! Put your head back and close your eyes or read a book.

For a shower or bath :

- Wash with soap.
- Wash all over, including hidden areas.
- Rub elbows, heels and tops of toe joints with loofa sponge.
- Brush cuticles with nail brush (fingers and toes).
- Shave underarms and legs.
- Rinse with cool water to close pores.
- Push back cuticles with manicure stick.
- Pat skin dry.
- Apply lotion.
- Powder will help you stay cool in the summer.
- Use deodorant.
- If you use perfume, use sparingly.
- Polish the chrome fixtures dry.
- Remove any hair on the floor of the shower or tub.
- Hang up towel and washcloth.
- Pick up bathroom. Your mother will give you a big kiss for this.

FACIAL CLEANSING

Wash your face twice a day to remove dirt, make-up and dead cells by following the steps below.

- Pull hair back in headband or pony tail.
- Wash your hands.
- Use a cleansing cream or soap, depending on your skin type and whether or not you use makeup.
- Deodorant soaps dry the skin. Use a non-deodorant, unscented soap. Work up a sudsy lather in your hands, first.
- Apply soap or cream gently to your face and neck. Use upward and outward strokes. Wash gently. Harsh rubbing can irritate your skin and damage the delicate area around your eyes.
- Rinse with warm water.
- When wearing makeup, gently remove with a kleenex or facial pad first. Then rinse with a warm washcloth. Why use a kleenex first? 1)You won't stain the washcloth and 2)Unless you plan on using a clean washcloth every day, you will be rubbing makeup from the washcloth back onto your face.
- Splash cool water on your face to close your pores.

FACIAL TONING

Use a toner (no alcohol) or astringent. This liquid lifts the last layer of dirt and neutralizes excess oil. This step will help keep blackheads and pimples away.

FACIAL MOISTURIZER

This will help seal in moisture on your face. Use after the toner or astringent and before you apply makeup. If you don't wear makeup, this will be your last step. Wear a night cream at night if you have dry skin.

SPECIAL FACIAL TREATMENTS

FACIAL SCRUBS

These creams contain some abrasives and help to remove dead cells and stimulate circulation. Use 1-2 times a week. If just your nose tends to be flaky, then apply to your nose and wipe off gently with a wet washcloth. Astringent should follow.

MASQUE

This treatment is used for deep cleansing. You can buy a masque product or make your own out of powdered milk or oatmeal. When using oatmeal, grind some in a food processor to make a fine powder first. Add enough water to the powdered milk or powdered oatmeal to make a paste.

The masque is applied and allowed to dry. Never masque around the delicate skin around your eyes or mouth. When removing the masque, first splash the face with warm water, softening the hardened masque. Then use a warm wet washcloth to remove the masque completely. Be careful not to stretch the skin on your face.

STEAM CLEANING

Fill a sink with boiling water. Bend over the sink and put a towel over your head to form a tent. Let the steam hit your face for at least five minutes. A wet washcloth warmed in the microwave works, too. Make sure you don't burn the cloth and that it is not too hot on your face.

Steam cleaning can relieve a sinus headache.

Steam cleaning makes your face feel cleaner. This technique, however, can have adverse affects on your skin. Just as humidity often spurs on facial eruptions, steam cleaning makes oily skin more prone to forming pimples and encourages bacteria in pores.

Steam clean once a month if you enjoy this method for making your face feel better. Don't use this technique on a regular basis, especially if you are prone to acne.

HAND AND NAIL CARE

LOVELY HANDS

Have you looked at your hands lately? What do you see? Are they rough and dry? Do they look older than the rest of your body? What about your cuticles? Are they creeping up your nails? Are your nails like stubs because of chewing on them? Do you have hangnails?

Forget trying to hide your hands. You need them to eat, greet people, wave good-bye, open doors, take a test ... Some of us talk with our hands, too. I cannot talk to anyone without using mine. People *will* notice your hands, so you might as well learn how to take care of them.

Plastic surgeons can do wonders with a face and other body parts to make them look younger and better. They cannot do a thing about hands, I'm afraid. So begin taking care of them now. There are no trade-ins.

NAIL CARE

Nails don't have to be long or polished, but they do have to be manicured. A proper diet will help your nails to be healthy. Detergents, chlorine in pools, weather, or a vitamin or iron deficiency can cause them to be soft or brittle.

Nails are very porous so they absorb water. When they dry out, they lose the water and split or peel. Keeping hands dry by wearing gloves when washing dishes, the family car, your dog ... will help keep your nails from becoming brittle. You can also rub a moisturizer or oil on them.

HOME MANICURE

Here is what you need:

- Polish remove
- Cotton balls
- Emery board
- Bowl filled with warm, soapy water
- Nail brush
- Cuticle cream
- Manicure stick
- Toothpick
- Hand towel
- Nail strengthener or base coat
- Nail polish
- Polish sealer
- Quick-dry, electric dryer, or baby oil

1) Remove old polish with cotton ball, dipped in polish remover.
2) File your nails towards the center and in one direction.
3) Soak one hand for five minutes.
4) After soaking one hand, clean nails and scrub cuticles with nail brush.
5) Towel dry nails.
6) Massage nails with cuticle cream and soak again.
7) Gently push back cuticles with manicure stick.
8) Repeat steps 3-7 on your other hand.
9) Lotion hands, keeping lotion off of nails.
10) Mend nail tears with nail glue.
11) Apply base coat or nail strengthener. Allow to dry five minutes.
12) Apply a coat of nail polish, using long strokes. Wipe off tip of nail so polish won't chip.
13) Apply a second coat. Let dry.
14) Apply a sealer coat.
15) Steps 10-13 can be eliminated and you can apply one coat of clear nail polish, instead.

Treat your cuticles gently. Pushing them back too far or without first softening them can cause damage. By breaking the seal of the cuticle, water gets underneath and can cause an infection.

Bruising cuticles through a minor trauma or cutting or damaging them causes whites ripples or spots on the nails. A white line in the same location in every nail indicates damage to the base of the nail, an abnormality in the body, such as a fever or past illness, or lost weight. Remove all nail polish before visiting a doctor. He will want to check your nails for signs of body dysfunctions.

Never wear chipped nail polish out of the house.

Lotion your hands every time they have been in water. This includes when you wash your hands after you go to the bathroom.

Lotion your hands before you go to bed, massaging the lotion into the cuticles.

Now that you know how to care for your hands and nails, will you use them as flags to wave around and show off, expecting to be complimented? Do not become conceited. Use your lovely hands to reach out to others.

Your lovely hands can be helpful at home, school, church, your neighborhood, wherever you happen to be. Your hands can welcome a new student to class or comfort a hurting friend.

Your lovely hands will never want to pick up magazines or books that are not becoming of a lady. They will not want to take part in the destruction of personal property, such as writing on walls. They will not be used to destroy property or your body, through the use of drugs.

Your lovely hands are to be used to do lovely things. Start by giving yourself a hug with your lovely hands.

YOUR FEET
Be kind to your feet so they will always want to take you wherever you want to go. During the summer, your feet will be in full view for

everyone to see. You will be wearing sandals or going barefoot at the pool and beach. You will want them to look soft, neat and clean.

Take care of your feet in the same way you take care of your hands. Keep your nails clipped. Your toe nails should be clipped and filed straight across to avoid ingrown toenails. Every time you finish bathing or showering, push those cuticles back while they are soft.

A loofa sponge or pumice stone is great for rubbing (gently!) away dry skin on your heels, the balls of your feet, and the tops of your toes. Use your loofa sponge while your feet are wet and lathered.

Your feet love to be lotioned, massaged and powdered. Any powder with starch will feed bacteria and cause an odor, so don't use it.

Buffing your nails or using clear nail polish makes your nails look attractive. During application, you can use toe separators or cotton balls to prevent the nail polish from rubbing off on toes that overlap.

Now that your feet look lovely, be kind to them. Wear shoes that fit properly and that have good support. Wear socks or panty hose with your shoes so that your feet can breathe.

Exercise your feet by rolling them back and forth over a can. Walk around on the balls of your feet. During your shower, you can stretch up on the balls of your feet and then relax. Repeat several times. You can do this while you brush your teeth as well. I love to combine exercise with another activity.

Now you know how to take care of your skin from head to toe. Be committed. Be diligent. Watch for wonderful results!

MORE HELPFUL HINTS

♠   Wash make-up brushes with shampoo and then put a conditioner on them like you would your own hair or they will dry out. Use only natural hair brushes because they are softer and easier to clean.

♠   To smooth a rough cuticle, file with an emery board.

♠ Quick-dry nails by rapidly running them under cold water or applying baby oil with a cotton-tip applicator.

♠ All-vegetable shortening is recommended by dermatologists to soften dry skin. After a shower or bath, apply to arms and legs that have been blotted with a towel (not completely dried).

♠ Keep a travel toothbrush with you so you can clean your teeth after meals when away from home.

♠ Breath test: After flossing, sniff the floss. Although the floss will smell stronger than your mouth, a foul odor indicates the need for improved oral hygiene habits immediately.

♠ Use only sugar-free breath fresheners. Bacteria act on sugar and produce an acid that causes decay and plaque.

♠ Ladies, use an oil free, water-based makeup. Apply only a light application.

♠ Deodorants are more effective on cool, dry skin. Do not apply right after your shower. Cool down first.

♠ For soft, attractive eyebrows, use eye shadow (in a shade close to your natural brow color) feathering in and following brow line. Rub a stiff brush, such as a toothbrush, across the powdered shadow, then brush the brow upward.

REVIEW
Skin Care

1. Does eating a balanced diet affect your health and body growth?
   Yes or No

2. Where should you apply sun block besides on your face? ("Skin Protection") _____

3. To protect your hands, wear gloves for household chores, _____, cold weather, and sports. The invisible glove is _____.

4. Skin around your _____ is the thinnest, so be gentle when cleansing and wear _____ for protection from the sun. ("Facial Image")

5. Wash your face at least _____ a day. After physical exertion, wash it again.

6. Before bathing, trim your _____ ("Skin and Cleanliness")

7. Nails for ladies don't have to be long or polished. Young men and ladies should keep their nails _____.

8. Why do your feet prefer that you wear socks with your shoes? ("Your Feet") _____

9. _____ are more effective on cool, dry skin. Do not apply right after your shower. Cool down first. ("Helpful Hints")

10. _____ Give yourself or someone else a manicure.

Dear Parent,

Teach your son or daughter that skin care involves more than daily cleansing. Proper cleansing, diet, fresh air, exercise, and skin protection each play an important role in promoting healthy, pleasant-looking skin.

As with other skills in this book, teach your son or daughter one step at a time. Perhaps, start at the top with facial cleansing and care, working down towards the hands with a manicure, a pedicure for the feet, and then over-all skin care and protection. You might prefer to let your child select an area of skin care more interesting to him/her. Young ladies usually enjoy focusing on home manicures. Give your son/daughter time to practice newly acquired skills before learning new ones.

Take your special son or daughter shopping to buy the necessary supplies listed in this chapter to help achieve a healthy skin care program. Teach him/her how to use these items properly as well as where to store them.

How your son or daughter treats his skin today determines the condition of his skin for tomorrow.

Deborah Wuerslin

LIFE LINE
Implementing Excellence

Personal Style

He knows about everyone, everywhere. Everything about us is bare and wide open to the all-seeing eyes of our living God; nothing can be hidden from him to whom we must explain all that we have done.
Hebrews 4:13 Living Bible

A man who refuses to admit his mistakes can never be successful. But if he confesses and forsakes them, he gets another chance.
Proverbs 28:13 Living Bible

For I know the plans I have for you, declares the Lord, plans to prosper you and not to harm you, plans to give you hope and a future.
Jeremiah 29:11 NIV

You can learn how to wear clothes to hide you physical imperfections, but what about your spiritual flaws? You cannot hide your spiritual imperfections from God. He knows and sees everything about you, and thru Christ, He accepts you as you are. He works in your life to make you unique and complete in many ways. (James 1:4)

Don't separate yourself from God through sin. Through Jesus Christ, confess anything in your life that displeases Him. God forgives you. It was His idea to provide forgiveness, restored fellowship, and guidance.

In your "quest for excellence" in your appearance as a godly young man and young woman, also ask God to continually work on your inner self. He will reshape your life into what He desires for you. Personality includes spiritual, mental, social, and physical dimensions. Luke 2:52 states, "And Jesus grew in wisdom, stature, and with favor with God and man."

His Word, His Spirit, and His daily promises are yours for personal growth as God daily cultivates in you His character and godly characteristics. *But we christians have no veil over our faces;we can be mirrors that brightly reflect the glory of the Lord. And as the spirit of the Lord works within us, we become more and more like Him.*

2 Corinthians 3:18 Living Bible

The person who is wrapped up in himself is generally overdressed.
Unknown

PERSONAL STYLE

WHAT IS PERSONAL STYLE?

Personal style is how you dress, how you carry yourself (posture), how you think and speak, and how you treat others. You will develop your own personal style by finding role models, people you will desire to borrow ideas from.

Your parents might be good examples of how to treat others. You might admire the way in which a certain teacher or pastor thinks. Maybe you like the way one of your parent's friends dresses. Your ballet teacher might be someone who gives you ideas on how to walk gracefully. Your coach represents good sportsmanship by not losing his temper over a bad call by a referee.

You will eventually develop your own unique style. I've dedicated this chapter to giving you ideas on developing your personal style in how you dress.

The clothes you wear, your personal style, tell people a lot about you -- your lifestyle, your personality, your attitude towards others, and how you perceive yourself. Are you confident? Gentlemen, is your positive self image reflected in the way you dress? Ladies, do you feel feminine?

Your choice of clothing affects your behavior. When you dress sloppily, you tend to feel sloppy. When you wear neat and clean clothes that complement you, your confidence shines through. Take pride in how you look. Learn how to be an individual without drawing attention to yourself.

The cost of your clothes is not the important issue. What counts is wearing clothes that fit, that are clean and that are mended. How you present yourself makes a difference in how people respond to you. The most beautiful dress or sharpest-looking outfit won't look appealing if you have poor posture, are not clean, and don't behave as a lady or gentleman.

FADS AND STYLES

In America, wearing name labels on clothing and accessories, such as handbags and shoes, is a fad. Yet in Europe, the average person cares about style more than fads. He or she wants to wear clothing of high, long-lasting quality. He will spend a lot of money on a briefcase or, she, a handbag, bearing no label because the quality of the leather is more important.

What is more important to you, fad or style? A fad interests people for a short time. Here are some fads from the past.

Mid 50's: Jeweled eye glasses were worn in a choice of colors.
              Young ladies wore the full "poodle" skirts.
              Men and boys wore "crew" cuts.
Late 60's: Hippie look: headbands and scarves were tied around the forehead.
Early 70's: Platform shoes and double knits.
Mid 80's: Men wore sport coat sleeves pushed up to the elbow.
Late 80's: Oversized tops with shoulder pads.
              Sneakers worn untied.
              Soft-leather tie loafers--"boat shoes."
Early 90's: Pants rolled up tightly at the ankles.
              No socks with shoes.

Fads can be fun, but you should not allow them to interrupt your personal style. You can wear a shawl or scarf tied around your neck, if that is the current fad, and still wear an outfit that fits your personal style. If bright, wild colors are the current fad, then wear just a splash of it, perhaps in your accessories. Make sure that you wear the fad while it is current. Don't wait to buy an article of clothing or an accessory as it is going out of style.

If a style or fashion is handed down from generation to generation, it becomes a custom. In the early 1800's, men traded their knee-high trousers for long pants. Today, it is a custom for men to wear long pants in most parts of the world. Pant styles have changed over the years, but the custom of wearing long pants remains.

WHAT IS YOUR PERSONAL STYLE IN HOW YOU DRESS?

Perhaps your style is to wear dressy clothes, or maybe you feel more comfortable in casual attire. Your personal style might be to mix and match clothes to keep people guessing what combination you are going to come up with next. Tailored clothes could be your style, preferring simple clothes with simple lines. The feminine look is another style for ladies, putting into play ruffles, lace, soft fabrics, and subtle prints. Some males and females enjoy wearing the sporty look. Whatever your look, be proud of being a lady or a gentleman of confidence.

Developing a trademark can be fun. Pat Boone, a singer and movie star, always wore white shoes. You may not find that appealing. Maybe you'll choose to wear one special cologne or interesting hats. Perhaps you have a special piece of jewelry to wear. You might not choose a trademark that sets you apart from others; it might just slowly develop. I never set out to buy or make a lot of clothes trimmed with lace. As I developed my own personal style, however, I discovered that many of my clothes were trimmed with lace. I realized that lace helped to give me the soft, feminine look which made me feel comfortable.

PUTTING YOURSELF TOGETHER

People come in all shapes and sizes: tall, short, thin, plump, big boned and small, small and large busts, wide and narrow hips and bulges in all sorts of places.

Exercises can trim a pudgy body, but there are some physical features you can do nothing about. If you are short, you cannot stretch your body. If you are tall, walking around with slumped shoulders only draws attention to your height.

First, look in a mirror to see what your best features are and wear clothes that focus your attention on these good features. "Accentuate the positive." If you have a small waist, wear something that shows off your waist.

Next, look at the areas on your body that are not your best features. This is not a condemnation but just being realistic. We all have figure flaws - - parts of our body that we wish were bigger or smaller, taller or shorter.

Fortunately, we can learn to wear clothes that hide what we don't like or at least minimize their appearance.

At the end of the "For Boys Only" and "For Girls Only" sections of Personal Style, are charts listing clothes and accessories for different figure types. Learn which styles look best on you. Fill most of your wardrobe with simple, basic styles. When you add something that is a fad, don't spend too much money on it. Style should be your priority, adding only a few fad items here and there.

Discover which colors look best on you. Certain colors will complement your hair, eyes and skin tone more than others.

BE PRACTICAL

Choose outfits that fit your lifestyle. If you never step foot off a farm, then a silk dress or pinstripe suit is not for you. Wearing short skirts may be a cute style but impractical if you have to go up and down stairs or sit on a floor in a daycare center to care for children. Dress according to what makes you feel comfortable for your activity.

DRESS FOR YOUR AGE

Trying to dress to look older than you are will only call attention to how young you are. Look through fashion magazines and catalogues for current styles for your age group.

DRESS FOR THE OCCASION

Americans have forgotten how to dress properly for different functions. Tennis shorts are great to wear on the courts (Wouldn't a formal or tuxedo look silly?), but they are inappropriate for the dentist's office. When going to church or the theatre, a lovely dress or coat and tie is in order, not jeans.

Boys, a necktie worn to a job interview, gives the interviewer the impression of your being a dependable worker. Wear clean, casual clothes when applying for a job as a manual laborer. When attending a baby or wedding shower, ladies, you should wear a dress or at least an attractive skirt and blouse. Your message to the honored guest is that you took a few extra minutes to look your best and to make her feel special.

> When I was in my early 20's, I took a part-time job as a bank teller. After only one month on the job, the bank manager offered me a promotion. He offered me this position over men and women who had been with the bank much longer than I. My supervisor told me that my skills were excellent, I was a dedicated worker, and I *dressed for the part*. I did not come to work in tight fitting slacks or sloppy clothes. I always looked professional wearing my neat, clean, and properly-fitted dresses. My appearance helped to give the bank a positive image.

"Black Tie" on an invitation means a dinner jacket or tuxedo worn with a black bow tie. The dinner jacket may be dark blue, black, brocade or plaid for the daring dresser, or a white jacket for summer. Ladies wear a short dinner dress or a long formal gown, depending on the occasion. Remember to complement your outfit with coordinating shoes, jewelry, and purse.

"Black Tie Optional," appearing more frequently on invitations to include all classes of people, enables men to wear a blue business suit and ladies a day or "church" dress. Couples will feel more comfortable wearing complementary outfits, either both wearing formal attire or their "Sunday best."

"White Tie," not worn often these days, requires a man to wear a tailcoat and a white pique tie and a lady to wear a dressy formal gown.

Don't overdress. Wearing a lot of jewelry to an aerobics class or on a hike in the mountains is showy and out of place. Wearing super dressy clothes on the job gives the idea that you are out to "impress" and not work seriously.

> Once on a date, my husband took me hiking in the mountains in Colorado. I thought I looked so cute in my orange wool turtle-neck sweater, wool slacks and hair ribbons wrapped around my long pigtails. During a break, Tom asked me why I was so dressed up. A sweatshirt and jeans, he said, would have been more appropriate attire for climbing mountains. I was overdressed.

Use common "cents". If you live on a hamburger budget, then do not try to buy a steak. Always try to buy quality but do not spend more money on clothes than your budget allows. Be a wise shopper and look for sales. Look for outlets. Learning to sew your own clothes is a wonderful way to show your creativity, to save money, and to have clothes that fit perfectly.

When shopping sales, look for well-made garments -- evenly stitched hems, seams and zippers that don't pucker, plaids and stripes that match at seams and shoulders, collars that lie flat.

Turn to the appropriate sections in this chapter, "For Boys Only" or "For Girls Only" for personalized and helpful guidelines regarding your wardrobe.

FOR BOYS ONLY*******FOR BOYS ONLY********FOR BOYS ONLY

PERSONAL STYLE

A PROPER FITTING

Select clothes for fit rather than size. Manufacturers vary on label sizes. Tight-fitting clothes or outfits too large for your size and body shape detract from the positive appearance you desire to reflect. Move around in any clothes you intend to buy, making sure they feel comfortable as well as fit properly.

Pants: The waist remains horizontal all the way around. The crotch not too tight or too baggy, should allow for free movement. The pant length, touching the top of the shoe, creates a break in the crease. The back length is even with the front on cuffed pants and 1/2"--3/4" longer than the front on pants without cuffs.

Jacket: The neck lies flat with no wrinkles. The chest fits with no wrinkles and tapers in at the waist for a thin person. The jacket length completely covers the rear end. The sleeve hangs 5 to 5 1/2" off the tip of the thumb. The jacket is meant to fit comfortably only for standing and basic movements. If making big movements, such as dancing, unbutton the coat or take it off.

Shirt: The collar is too tight when it wrinkles and too big when more than two fingers can slide up and down between the shirt and your neck. Your shirt should not be baggy at the waist, but long enough so it does not pull out of your pants with movement. The end of the shirtsleeve falls just below the wrist bone.

DRESS MODESTLY

The way you dress affects your behavior. American Indian warriors once covered their faces with "warpaint" to make themselves feel fierce as well as terrify their enemies. Street gangs cover themselves with tattoos and wear all black attire, draped with heavy chains, to intimidate people.

Boys who unbutton their shirts to their navels send ungentlemanly signals to girls. Their clothes can attract the wrong type of people and scare off others who might be a positive influence in their lives.

Keep your accessories simple.

Belts: A reversible black/brown belt matches most of your pants. Keep the belt buckle small and simple.

Glasses: Allow a professional to help you select glasses that complement your eyes and face shape. Wear sunglasses with ultra-violet protection, taking them off when indoors.

Hats: Hats are stylish to wear and shade your eyes from the bright sun, keeping your head warm in cold temperatures. Baseball and painters caps can coordinate or add a splash of color to a casual outfit. They look out of place, however, with a suit. Accessorize a casual outfit with casual accessories and a dressy outfit with dressy accessories. A gentleman removes his hat when indoors.

Jewelry: Too much jewelry makes a male seem unmanly and turns some people off. Necklaces on males are a fad and not acceptable in the business world. A handful of rings draws a person's focus to your hands. One ring on each hand is sufficient. One ring period is best.

Socks: Always wear socks with shoes and change them daily. White cotton socks effectively absorb sweat for sports and exercise. Wear dark colored socks for dress. Match either your shoes or pants. Don't wear patterned socks with patterned pants.

Shoes: Your shoes don't have to match the color of your outfit but should match in style. Wear dress shoes, usually in neutral colors made of leather, with a suit. Sneakers or boat shoes accompany casual outfits. Keep your leather shoes polished and sneakers clean. Replace worn laces.

Ties: Ties add the finishing touch to an outfit. A tie can be colorful but not gaudy. Ties with prints and patterns look best with solid shirts. When tied properly, the tip of the tie should touch your belt buckle. Avoid wearing short ties.

1) Start with the wide end of the tie on your right, extending a foot below the narrow end.

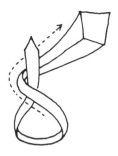

2) Cross the wide end over the narrow and turn back underneath.

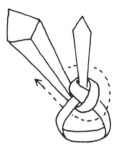

3) Bring up and turn down through the loop.

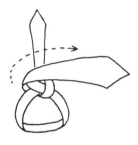

4) Pass the wide end around the front from left to right.

5) Then, up through the loop.

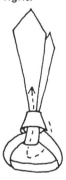

6) Pull down through the knot in front. Tighten carefully and draw up to the collar.

Of the three methods for tying a tie, the most popular is the half-Windsor knot. This method makes a symmetrical triangle for standard shirt collars. The other two methods include the Windsor knot and the four-in-hand knot. The half-Windsor knot is shown in the illustration.

Umbrellas: Men carry black umbrellas, saving the floral designs for females.

Underwear: Don't wear colored underwear under white or pastel pants. Wear round-necked undershirts under a shirt and tie and V-necked under an open collar.

Wallets: Don't stuff it so full that it bulges from your pants pocket.

Watches: More of an essential item to remind you of the time, watches come in all shapes and sizes. When your budget allows, wear a dress watch to complement a suit. At your age, a more casual watch is acceptable.

Remember to turn off the hourly signal of digital watches when in quiet places such as the theatre, church, and the classroom.

Care about every detail in how you dress. Dress conservatively, not combining more than two patterns or wearing colors that clash. Dress in a style you feel comfortable in without drawing undo attention to your outer appearance. Respect school and work dress codes, as well as the wishes of your parents.

Show appreciation for the clothes you have by keeping your clean clothes hung up or neatly folded and put away. Take care of your clothes by washing them when soiled, ironing them when wrinkled, and mending them when torn.

Before you leave the house, check your appearance:
    1) Is my hair clean and brushed?
    2) Are my face, neck, and ears clean?
    3) Do I need to shave?
    4) Are my nails clean and neatly trimmed?

5) Am I wearing the appropriate color and style of underwear?

6) Do I have any hanging threads that need clipping?

7) Do I have any missing or hanging buttons?

8) Do I have any seams that need mending?

9) Is every zipper zipped and every button buttoned?

10) Is my shirt label sticking up and showing at my neckline?

11) Is my shirt tucked in?

12) Is my belt twisted?

13) Are my shoes polished and repaired and laces not frayed?

14) Do I have spots on my clothes?

15) Do my clothes need ironing?

16) Am I dressed for the occasion?

DRESSING TO MAKE YOU LOOK YOUR VERY BEST

SHORT

- Vertical (up and down) stripes, long lines, and stitching.
- Single colors add the illusion of length (matching shirt and pants or jackets and pants).
- Only small prints.
- Suspenders.
- Narrow ties.
- No cuffs on pants.

LARGE BUILD

- Vertical lines.
- Well-fitting clothes, neither too loose nor too tight.
- Wear simple clothes with a tailored look.
- Avoid loud, gaudy clothes. (Sales people tell large customers they can get away with this, but loud clothes only draw attention to your large size.)
- Avoid pleated pants.
- Dark or neutral, single-color outfits. If you are tall, you can wear a light top with a dark bottom.

- Narrow ties.
- Suspenders.

TALL

- Horizontal lines.
- Large prints and bold stripes.
- Contrasting colors (green shirt and navy pants) breaks up your height.
- Thick bulky fabrics.
- Think big -- belts, pockets, collars, sweaters, and accessories.
- Cuffs on jackets and pants (to cut height).

SLENDER

- Tall and slender, wear same styles as for tall person.
- Average height, wear horizontal lines.
- Loose-fitting clothes or the layered look, avoiding tight-fitting clothes.
- Light and bright colors.
- Bright prints and plaids.
- Double-breasted jackets.

Being legalistic about your wardrobe limits your selection. A gentleman with a thin build, for example, doesn't have to stick to loose-fitting clothes or horizontal stripes. He can wear anything he chooses. Just knowing what complements your figure type brings confidence. Wear whatever styles you desire but aiming to look your best by following the guidelines above.

OTHER HELPFUL HINTS

- If shoes get wet, stuff them with newspaper or paper towels and allow them to dry away from heat.

- Hang a nylon stocking filled with cedar chips in the closet for a refreshing smell as well as a good moth repellent.

- Apply clear paste wax to protect the leather of boots.

♠ Rub a bar of soap on a metal zipper to make it slide easier.

♠ Hang sport coats and jackets on padded hangers to avoid hanger marks at the shoulders.

♠ Empty the pockets in your pants before hanging them up on the proper hanger.

♠ Never put two patterns next to each other.

♠ A gentleman removes his hat when indoors.

FOR GIRLS ONLY*******FOR GIRLS ONLY******FOR GIRLS ONLY

PERSONAL STYLE

FIT AND PROPER

Make sure your clothes fit. Buy according to fit not size. One designer's size eight may be smaller than another's size eight. If your outfit is even a tiny bit too big, have it altered. If the hem is even one inch too long, hem it. The proper adjustments will change the total look of your outfit. Although no one may notice that your dress fits properly, they will notice if it does not.

DRESS MODESTLY

Clothing should not be too tight or too low cut in the front. Bend over in front of the mirror to make sure that no one can see your bra. A sheer blouse should have a camisole (the top half of a slip) or a full slip under it. Immodest dressing attracts the wrong type of admirer.

Make sure that accessories complement and coordinate with your outfit. If you wear a fancy outfit, wear dressy jewelry like pearls or a gold necklace. Wear costume jewelry, like plastic beads, with casual wear. Do not wear costume jewelry with a dressy outfit even if it matches in color. Do not wear a cheap belt on a good dress. You can, however, wear a good quality belt on an inexpensive dress.

Do not mix your jewelry Wear gold with gold and silver with silver. Your wedding ring, the only exception, does not have to match.

One ring on each hand is adequate. Better to wear too little jewelry than too much. Wearing too much jewelry will detract from you and your outfit.

If you wear an unusual and attractive necklace, then wear a small, simple belt. Choose your accessories that do not compete with one another.

Your shoes do not have to match the color of your outfit but should match in style. Sneakers do not go with a lovely dress. Heels should not be worn with slacks.

If you wear knee high hose with a skirt, the tops of them will probably show when you sit down or climb stairs.

Your wardrobe should include a variety of lingerie (under clothing). You might need a variety of bras (sweater bra, strapless, low waisted) for different outfits.

You will definitely need several styles and lengths of slips. A short slip under a long skirt will be noticed when you stand in the light. When you wear a straight skirt, you want to wear a straight slip. A full slip would bunch up and give your straight skirt a puckered appearance.

If you wear a sheer blouse with slacks, then wear a camisole (the top part of a slip) under your blouse. A young woman of confidence of loveliness does not allow anyone to see her underclothing through her clothes. A cotton knit camisole in cold weather provides extra warmth.

Did you know that lingerie the color of your skin is better to wear under clothing? White lingerie will separate from your skin tone and will show through.

If you try to wear bikini underwear under slacks, your panty line will show. Wear briefs under slacks. Make sure that your underwear has a cotton panel. Cotton breathes and is more healthful.

Care about every detail in the way you dress. If you were making a cross-stitch picture for a friend, you would make sure that every part of the picture was *neatly* stitched. Dress yourself in the same manner. Pretend you are a gift to yourself.

Before I leave the house, I will always check the following to make sure that my appearance is neat:
1) Is my hair clean and brushed?
2) Are my face, neck and ears clean?
3) Is my makeup well blended and any excess removed?
4) Do I need to shave my underarms or legs?
5) Is my nail polish chipped?
6) Does my bra or panty line show through my clothes?
7) Does my slip show at the hem?

8) Does a bra or slip strap show at the neckline or armhole?

9) Is my slip too short?

10) Are my pantyhose snagged or sagged?

11) Do the reinforced toes on my pantyhose peep out of open-toe shoes?

12) Is my skirt centered?

13) Do I have any loose or missing buttons?

14) Do I have any threads showing?

15) Do I have any seams that need mending?

16) Do I have any spots on my clothes?

17) Is my belt twisted?

18) Is the clothing label sticking up and showing at my neckline?

19) Are my shoes polished and repaired?

20) Is every button buttoned and zipper zipped?

21) Do my clothes need ironing?

22) Am I dressed for the occasion?

DRESSING TO MAKE YOU LOOK YOUR BEST

SHORT

- Vertical (up and down) stripes, long lines, pleats and stitching.
- If long hem lines are in style, wear yours slightly shorter. Do not wear mini skirts, either. Your clothes need to be in proportion (balanced).
- Think small -- belts, pockets, collars, and accessories including a medium to small purse).
- Narrow or slightly-flared skirts.
- Single colors are best. Only small prints.
- Short vests and jackets.

SLIGHTLY HEAVY OR WIDE HIPS

- Vertical lines.
- Well-fitting clothes, neither too loose or too tight.
- Wear simple clothes with a tailored look.
- Flared skirts (avoid pleated skirts and pleated pants).
- Longer skirt hemlines.
- Full-sleeved blouses to offset wide hips.

- Dark or neutral, single-color outfits. If you are tall, you can wear a light top with a dark bottom.
- Large jewelry.

TALL

- Horizontal lines look good.
- Large prints and bold stripes.
- Contrasting colors (red blouse with a navy skirt) breaks up your height.
- Think big -- belts, pockets, collars, sweaters, and accessories. You can carry an oversized purse.
- Full skirts.
- Three-quarter length jackets.

SLENDER

- If you are tall and slender, wear same styles as for tall person.
- If you are average, wear horizontal lines.
- Loose-fitting clothes or the layered look. Avoid tight-fitting clothes.
- Light and bright colors.
- Bright prints and plaids.
- Double-breasted jackets.
- Ruffles.

SMALL BOSOM

- Loose-fitting tops.
- Blouses with front pockets or pleats.
- Blouses with ruffles or ties.

LARGE BOSOM

- Tops with vertical lines.
- Tops darker than bottoms.
- V-necked or scooped-necked tops.
- Scarf or neck ruffle to draw attention away from bosom.
- Light-weight or medium fabrics.

Do not be too legalistic about your wardrobe. No law says that a short person, for example, has to wear single-color outfits to make her look taller. When you have confidence, you can wear anything you want. Just knowing what looks best on you will give you confidence. When you have your picture taken or speak before an audience, then you might want to stick to the clothes that look best for your specific figure type.

Don't make your wardrobe the center of your attention. Remember that your smile, your posture, your hair, a neat appearance, and a sweet disposition all work together in making an attractive you.

OTHER HELPFUL HINTS

♠ Wear the solid-color jacket from a suit over one of your print dresses. You have created a new look.

♠ Put your pantyhose on before your jewelry, so your nylons will stay snag free.

♠ When hand washing lingerie, add a drop of your favorite cologne in the final rinse to surround you in scent.

♠ Be creative with your accessories. Use pierced earrings as pins. Fasten a neck scarf with a decorative barrette.

♠ Plan what you are going to wear the night before, after you check the weather report. You'll have time to experiment with colors and accessories and combine new looks.

REVIEW
Personal Style

1. What was one of the fads worn in the mid 50's? _____
    _____

2. What is an example of a trademark someone might choose to wear?
    _____

3. When buying an outfit, consider what colors look best on you, your lifestyle, your _____, and the occasion. ("Putting Yourself Together")

4. When purchasing clothes, buy according to _____ not size. ("Fit and Proper")

5. Make sure that _____ complement and coordinate with your outfit.

6. Ladies, your wardrobe needs several styles and lengths of
    _____

7. Under "Before I leave the house" in item 13 for boys and item 19 for girls, what should you check? _____
    _____

8. A girl short in statue should wear large or small prints? ("Dressing To Make You Look Your Best")

9. A male with a slender figure should wear loose or tight-fitting clothes? ("Dressing To Make You Look Your Best") _____

10. Although you know what styles of clothes look best on your body shape, don't become legalistic about the guidelines. Feel free to wear what you like; just know what looks best on you.

Dear Parent,

"Personal Style" helps you guide your son or daughter into dressing in a style suitable for his/her age, activities, budget, shape and size. Discuss current fads and how to incorporate them into his wardrobe in a tasteful manner. Go through your son's or daughter's wardrobe with him/her, discussing appropriate outfits for different occasions, accessorizing each one.

Teach your son or daughter how to follow the guidelines in this chapter. As he or she learns how to become comfortable with his/her appearance, a gentleman or young woman of confidence will begin to bloom.

Deborah Wuerslin

LIFE LINE
Implementing Excellence

Organizing Your Wardrobe

Lord, when doubts fill my mind, when my heart is in turmoil, quiet me and give me renewed hope and cheer.
Psalms 94:19 Living Bible

Regardless of the size of your wardrobe, thank the Lord for his provisions. Show your gratitude by taking care of your clothes and accessories.

We tend to think of "organization" and "routine" as boring. I trust that God will show you how your life can become liberated by routinely organizing your wardrobe. You will have more free time for activities you enjoy. You will, especially, feel accomplishment and satisfaction for properly taking care of your clothes.

God can replace a feeling of drudgery with one of joy. Instead of feeling sick every time you think of your closet and drawers, you will become challenged into thinking of new and creative ways of organizing your belongings, other than the tips I offer in this chapter.

Excellence is not an act...but a habit.
- Aristotle

ORGANIZING YOUR WARDROBE

Now that you know what clothes look best on you, you will want to know how to take care of them. You will also want to know how to organize your closet and drawers. Arranging your clothes in a particular order, will make your wardrobe seem larger. You will be able to mix and match your clothes easier.

Organize your closet before you open the closet door one day and everything falls on top of you. Organize your clothes before you are late for an appointment because you cannot find a particular outfit.

Before you begin, play some of your favorite music on the radio or stereo (nothing too slow). Lively music will help you to work in a more cheerful atmosphere and make the time pass more quickly.

EVERYTHING OUT
Vacuum and dust your empty closet. Could it use some paint or an attractive border? Do you have proper lighting?

Put all of your clothes in four stacks:

Stack One:
- Clothes you haven't worn in the past year.
- Clothes that don't fit.
Give these clothes to a relative, friend, or needy organization.

Stack Two:
- Clothes of Sentimental value.
- Clothes you might someday wear to a costume party.
Put these clothes in another closet or in a box in the attic or basement. Be sure to clean them first, as soiled clothes attract moths and insects. Add moth balls and label the box.

116

Stack Three:
- Off-season clothes.

Store these clothes the same way as Stack Two. If you have room, you may move your off-season clothes to the back of your closet and your in-season clothes to the front.

Stack Four:
- Clothes to go back in the closet.

LET'S GET ORGANIZED

There are different categories in which you can put your clothes in your closet:

1) Play, work, school or business, and party
2) Colors
3) Type of garment

I prefer to organize my clothes according to the type of garment, such as dresses, skirts, blouses, jackets, and slacks. Then I divide each category according to color. This includes all accessories: purses, belts, scarves and shoes.

Now the fun part begins. Put your clothes back in your closet in an organized manner. Separate a suit. Put the jacket with the jackets, the pants with the pants, and the skirt with the skirts. In this way, you will be more likely to mix and match your clothes.

Before you put a garment in the closet, make sure it doesn't need mending. If a button is loose, a seam tearing apart, or a hem hanging, repair it right away. Safety pins are cheating and someone will always see them.

Select the type of hanger you are to use.
Jackets on large wooden or padded hangers
Dresses on sturdy plastic or padded hangers
Blouses and shirts on lightweight plastic hangers
Skirts on skirt (clip) hanger
Pants on sturdy plastic or pant hangers

Don't use wire hangers. Clothes slide and wrinkle and they become easily entangled.

Have all of your clothes *face the same way* with zippers closed and at least one button buttoned.

Fold knits and sweaters and place on a closet shelf. They will stretch out of shape on a hanger.

Give your clothes *breathing space.* You don't want to smash and wrinkle them.

"OUT OF SIGHT, OUT OF MIND."

If you can't see something, you won't wear it. If you hang clothes in garment bags, leave the bags unzipped so you can see what is inside. If you have shoes in boxes, cut off the end of the box or label your shoe boxes. A different idea, yet, is to take a picture of each pair of shoes and attach each picture to the appropriate box. If you put sweaters in drawers, you won't see them and won't wear them. Stack them on a closet shelf.

Because of the humidity in parts of the country, storing clothes in plastic bags will cause them to stain or discolor. So protect off-season clothes from dust by covering them with sheets, pillow cases, or a large piece of cotton fabric. Cotton breathes and will discourage mildew. To keep dust off the shoulders of in-season clothing, you may use paper covers from the cleaners.

Shoes should be organized according to color and style (heels, flats, sneakers, slippers). Place them on a rack or on the closet floor, side by side or in boxes as mentioned above. Do your shoes need polishing? Do they need to go to the shoe repair shop? Shoes that are unpolished, dirty, or with worn-down heels will give you a sloppy look.

Purchase special hangers or racks for belts. These hangers also work well for scarves and necklaces. Cup or coat hooks, or a man's tie rack work well, also. Clothespins that clip, nailed to the wall, are great for hanging gloves and hats.

118

DRAWERS

Everything out! Organize in the same way you did with your closet clothes: tops in one drawer, shorts in another, pajamas in another...

For items such as underclothes and socks, drawer dividers help keep drawers neat. Remember to separate colors.

Keep pantyhose in the original containers. They will not snag in your drawer, and you will have all the needed information (brand name, size, color) to replace them.

QUICK FIXES

Keep safety pins on hand for mending emergencies. Better yet, keep a mini sewing kit in your room. "A stitch in time saves nine."

HOW FRESH!

Closet and drawer potpourri can add freshness to your room. You may purchase scented sachets or make your own. To make your own, buy some potpourri. Place a handful of it in a piece of fabric or lace. Delicate hankies of old-fashioned lace are so feminine. Tie the fabric or hankie with satin ribbon.

You can also spray cotton balls with your favorite cologne or aftershave and tie them up in attractive fabric. When the scent fades, open and spray the cotton again.

Here is how to help dehumidify your closet (taking extra moisture out of the air). Fill an empty coffee can with charcoal briquettes and punch holes in the lid. Set the can on a shelf or hang it from the ceiling. The charcoal will absorb the unwanted moisture in your closet. Keeping the lights on in your closet will also keep mildew from growing. This is a good idea to remember when you go on an extended summer vacation.

After you have organized your closet and drawers, take a few pictures. Tack these pictures up on your bulletin board or somewhere where you can see them. These pictures will help you to remember how neat you want to keep your room.

OTHER HELPFUL HINTS

♠ Multiple skirt and pant hangers are great space savers for off-season clothes.

♠ Color code socks to keep family members' socks separate. Each person has a different color sewn under the toes.

♠ Fold cords from curling irons, hot rollers, and blow dryers and place in empty toilet paper tubes. No more cord tangles!

♠ Polish your silver jewelry with toothpaste. You will save money by not having to use silver polish.

♠ Enhance your home with sachet. Tie sachets to headboards and bedposts. Tuck behind chair pillows. Place on bookshelves, bathroom countertops, and in the linen closet. Hang on clothes hangers and in garment bags. Place sachets in your drawers, stationery boxes, and clothes hamper.

♠ Keep shoes laces from continually coming untied by "misting" them with a spray bottle of water before tying.

♠ Accordian cup racks make great organizers for hats, belts, and scarves.

♠ Use a free evening, perhaps in front of the TV, to catch up on wardrobe maintenance: sew on buttons, mend split seams, fix hems, iron, polish shoes.

REVIEW
Organizing Your Wardrobe

1. After you take everything out of your closet, what should you do in your now empty closet? _____

2. List the four stacks in which you are to put your clothes:
      a)
      b)
      c)
      d)

3. Should all of your hangers in your closet match? Yes or No.

4. For a neater look, have all of your clothes face _____
_____. Zip zippers and button at least one button so the outfit does not fall off the hanger.

5. Storing clothes in plastic bags can cause clothes to _____ or
_____.

6. How can you keep family members' socks separate? ("Other Helpful Hints") _____

Dear Parent,

Help your son or daughter organize his/her clothes by following the guidelines in this chapter. Most young people dislike working alone and appreciate the input and company from a parent.

Maintaining a neat closet and drawers prevents major cleanings and sortings, although I do recommend a thorough cleaning and wardrobe appraisal every six months. If your son or daughter regularly "forgets" to put clothes in their proper place, monitoring will help set a daily routine. I suggest to the parents of my students to use the straightening up time (perhaps after dinner) as an opportunity for relationship building. Sit in your son's or daughter's room for about ten minutes and chit chat while he/she picks up. Tidying up seems less of a chore if he/she can share about activities, friendships, and feelings with you during this time.

This time of togetherness can continue through the years. I still enjoy my one-on-one talks with my children.

Deborah Wuerslin

LIFE LINE
Implementing Excellence

First Impressions

Kindness makes a man (and woman) attractive.
Proverbs 19:22 Living Bible

You gain confidence when you know how to handle yourself in social situations. Your friends enjoy your company because you do not become easily upset. They also appreciate your genuine concern for them.

Continue reaching out to others, focusing on making them feel comfortable in their surroundings. *Live in harmony with one another; be sympathetic, love as brothers (and sisters), be compassionate and humble.* 1 Peter 3:8 NIV

He who loves a pure heart, and whose speech is gracious, will have the king
for his friend.
Proverbs 22:11 NIV

FIRST IMPRESSIONS

When you learn how to handle yourself in different social situations, you will not need to feel awkward, shy or even stupid. You will be prepared to respond quickly and naturally. When a situation arises in which you are uncertain how to act, you will have enough confidence to do your best and keep smiling.

This chapter will teach you how to introduce yourself to others. After the basic introduction is made, you will learn effective ways to start a conversation and to keep it running smoothly. The super quiet person will no longer embarrass you by his or her silence because you will have learned how to get that person to talk to you.

You will begin to put your shyness aside and step out to talk to others. Speaking in public and talking on the telephone will be easier for you because of your new confidence. Your confidence will spread to others like sunshine on a rainy day.

Have you ever been walking down the sidewalk with a friend and have your friend meet someone who she knows? What did your friend do? Did she chat merrily along with her other friend, leaving you just standing alone, feeling left out? What should your friend have done? What could you have done?

After greeting her other friend, your friend should have introduced the two of you and included you in the conversation.

Perhaps your friend does not know how to make introductions. Rather than just standing there, wait for a pause in their conversation, and introduce yourself to the other friend. Do not be pushy, however. If there is no pause, forget the introduction and cheerfully say good-bye as you and your friend continue your walk. After you are out of earshot of the other friend, you may ask who that person was.

Now that you know how left out you feel when not introduced, let me teach you the proper way to make an introduction. Your friends will appreciate you for being such a thoughtful friend to always introduce them to anyone they might not know.

An introduction can be the presentation of one person to another individual or to a group, or yourself to another person or persons. I like to think of an introduction as the salutation to a letter. Rather than jumping right in with a letter to someone, you would begin, for example, with "Dear Susan." Don't wait for two people who do not know each other to just start talking. First introduce them to one another.

Your introductions should always be friendly and with a smile. Remember your body language. If you act embarrassed, your friends are going to feel awkward. Eye contact and good posture will show your confidence.

Generally speaking, your introductions will fall into one of five groups.

Group One: Person with Title

A principal, a teacher, a doctor, a senator, a judge are examples of people with titles. Say the name of the person with the title, first. "Judge Fairly, this is my father, David Jones. Dad, this is Judge Fairly."

Group Two: Lady

When introducing a girl to a boy or a woman to a man, say the female's name first. "Diane, this is Michael Manly. Michael, this is Diane Dimples."

When a young lady turns 16, she falls under group two as a lady rather than group three as a young person. For example, although your father is older, you would mention your 16 year old girlfriend's name first. "Shannan, this is my father, Mr. Burton. Dad, this is Shannan Burnett." Your father is the one to decide whether or not he is to have your friend call him by his first name.

Group Three: Older Person

Say the older person's name, first. "Mom, this is Jeff Smith. Jeff, this is my mother, Mrs. Thornburgh." If your mother's last name is different from yours, your friend will know the proper name to use. Do not use an adult's first name, unless invited to do so. Even if you are over 16, wait for the invitation of, "Please call me, Deborah." When I meet a woman much older than I, I still wait for the invitation, especially someone with a title.

Group Four: Yourself

When introducing yourself to an individual, simple say, "Hello, I am Cindy Sokolik." If you are from out of town, say, "Hello, I am Cindy Sokolik from St. Louis."

Group Five: Individual to group

Say the name of the individual first. "Debbie Darling, these are my friends, Philip Fox, Beth Brave, and Jim Joker."

MAKING THE MOST OF YOUR INTRODUCTION

Is that all there is to an introduction? Not quite. Remember these additional rules:

Speak slowly and clearly.

SHAKE HANDS with the person to whom you are being introduced. A handshake is a sign of friendship. This custom has been "handed down" from the Middle Ages. When armed men approached each other, they would extend their empty hands as a sign of peace.

Say, "How do you do?" as soon as you have been introduced. Repeating the person's name right away will help you to remember it. "How do you do _____?"

If you do not understand the person's name, ask, "Excuse me, what was your name again?"

126

"Hey there, Diane."

"Hi, Diane. How're you doing?"
A firm grasp, smile and eye contact show confidence.

For young ladies under sixteen, always stand when being introduced to an adult and remain standing until they are seated or you are invited to do so. Everyone should stand when the guest of honor enters the room.

When making the introduction, tell your relationship to each person. "Linda, this is my friend Ed Edify, my neighbor. Ed, this is Linda Lovely from my gymnastics team."

Have you ever felt awkward after an introduction, not knowing what to say after, "How do you do?" Give a conversational starter. "Ed, this is my friend Linda Lovely from my gymnastics team. Linda, this is Ed Edify, my neighbor. Ed has just moved here from Alaska. He has lived all over the United States." Now Linda can respond with "Alaska! How interesting. Did you ever see any polar bears up close, and were you frightened if you did?" Share information that gives the people who are being introduced some interesting topics of conversation.

Forgotten a name? Everybody does once in awhile. Just say, "I'm sorry. I have forgotten your name."

Practice making introductions at home and with your friends so you feel relaxed when making real introductions. If you ever forget the rules, make the introduction anyway. Most people don't know the rules, but they will remember if you neglect to introduce them.

REVIEW
First Impressions

1. _____ Make three introductions this week and be prepared to share at least one of these in class. You may introduce family members, if necessary.

2. _____ Continue to practice good posture.

3. When you introduce your mother to your teacher, whose name do you mention first? _____

4.   Where   are   your   eyes   looking   when   greeting   someone?
_____

5. What do you do if you forget someone's name when making an introduction? _____

6. How can you help the people with whom you are introducing so they don't just stand in silence after saying, "How do you do?" _____
_____

7. When you are seated and someone wants to introduce you to an adult, what should you do?
_____

8. When you ignore introducing your friends to one another, how do you think they feel?
_____

9. When you ignore introducing your friends to your parents, how do you think your parents feel?
_____

First Impressions

Dear Parent,

Practicing introduction rules brings confidence. Role play with your son or daughter and encourage him/her to introduce their friends, teachers, and coaches to you.

As you teach your son or daughter how to make a positive first impression, emphasize friendliness over rules. Most people do not know the proper rules of introduction. They will remember, however, that a friendly and courteous introduction was made.

'Til we meet again.

Deborah Wuerslin

LIFE LINE
Implementing Excellence

CONVERSATIONS

A good man's speech reveals the rich treasures within him.
Matthew 12:35 Living Bible

Don't talk so much. You keep putting your foot in your mouth. Be sensible and turn off the flow!
Proverbs 10:19 Living Bible

Everyone should be quick to listen, slow to speak...
James 1:19

You can try to memorize kind sayings to share with people all day long, but if your heart isn't right in tune with the Lord, your speech will not reveal "treasures."

How do you make your heart more like our Lord's? Grow closer to him through daily prayer, reading God's Word, attending church and Sunday School, and fellowshipping with other Christians. When you are spiritually tuned in to station G-O-D, you won't have to memorize kind words. Love will overflow out of your mouth from your heart.

Listening is an important part of conversation and precedes responding. Others need understanding. Cultivate the art of listening and you will more easily learn how to respond to others, meet their needs, and develop deep lasting relationships. Friendships are built on trust, confidentiality, sharing, and learning to respond from the heart as well as the head.

Conversation is but carving;
Give no more to every guest
Than he's able to digest,
Give him always of the prime,
And a little at a time;
Give to all but just enough,
Let them neither starve nor stuff
And that each may have his due,
Let your neighbor carve for you.

Unknown

CONVERSATIONS

Showing yourself to be friendly is a good step towards making friends. Rather than waiting for someone to start a conversation, you start one. Treat all people with kindness. Do not prejudge someone and say, "She does not look like MY type. I think I will pass her by without saying anything."

I like to talk with people with interests other than mine as well as people who come from different places. Some of these people might not become my best friends, but I learn a lot about other people and places by talking with a variety of people.

I do not mean for you to go up to just anyone on the street and strike up a conversation. This is not always a safe thing to do. What about people at your school, church, or neighborhood? Go up to that shy person and say a few friendly words.

You can show kindness to adults, as well. Adults really enjoy a young person who takes the time to make conversation with them. A particular woman visiting our church returned the next Sunday because one of my children looked her in the eyes, shook her hand and said, "I am so glad you came today." You are special and YOU can make a difference in the lives of others.

An introduction is just a beginning to a conversation. Here are some helpful guidelines for having a successful conversation with someone.

- Have a pleasant voice, with a smile in it.

- Do not speak too fast or too slowly.

- Do not speak too loudly or too softly.

- Speak clearly. Good diction means taking the time to pronounce each word clearly, without exaggeration, of course.

- Be patient. Do not interrupt.

- Eye contact!

- Never use foul language. This not only offends people but also shows your lack of vocabulary.

- Do not use repetitive words and phrases; such as, "You know," "Okay," "Uh-huh," etc.

- Be honest.

- Be modest. Do not brag about yourself, but do not cut yourself down, either.

- Show respect for others. Always speak kindly of others.

- Do not talk about your personal, private or family matters.

- If you whisper in a conversation, someone else in the room will think that you are sharing bad news about him/her. If you have something private to share, wait until you and your friend are alone.

- Include everyone in a conversation. Talk about a subject that everyone understands.

Since a conversation is not just one person talking:

- Be a good listener. Do not do all of the talking, no matter how interesting you think you are to others. You will learn from others by listening to them.

- Give everyone in your group an opportunity to participate in the conversation.

- Respond to what a person is saying by asking a question or making a comment.

- How impolite to correct an adult!

- Rather than allowing your eyes to roam around the room, keep looking the person with whom you are speaking. Eye contact reflects a good listener.

- Do not fiddle with your hands, jewelry, clothing, or hair.

- No yawning!

GETTING STARTED

You might say, "I am too shy to start a conversation." Everyone is shy once in awhile. You CAN learn to deal with your shyness. Listing all of your positive personality traits will give you confidence. Here are some good traits to have. Perhaps you can think of others. There might be some in this list you would like to work on to become part of your positive personality trait list -- Interesting conversationalist, good listener, good sense of humor, patient, dependable, honest, hard worker, positive outlook on life, kind, respects others, generous, ...

Remember, you are special and have something to offer others.

CONVERSATION STARTERS are short comments or questions that will help you start a conversation. You can talk about:

- Vacation plans
- A new neighbor or classmate

- School - new teacher, extracurricular activity
- A fantastic new book
- An interesting hobby
- Make a sincere compliment
- Tell a good joke
- Share a bit of trivia
- Current events
- The weather, if you can't think of another topic

Try to pay attention to what is going on in the news. The newspaper will give you a more thorough report than television or the radio. Even though you will not remember everything and might not understand all, you will have a basic idea of what is going on around the world. My children have amazed adults about their knowledge of recent world events.

Start a conversation with a positive comment rather than a complaint. People enjoy hearing about your likes rather than hearing about your dislikes, and what you find interesting rather than your pet peeves.

- Use "You" a lot in your conversation rather than "I."

- Try not to stay on one subject for too long.

- Know your audience. If you get too technical for someone, he/she will not understand you and become bored.

- Do not try to force someone to have your same opinion. Share your feelings and facts and let them decide for themselves.

- Avoid depressing topics.

- If someone complains, turn it into something positive. "Rain. Rain. Rain. All we get is rain." Your response: "Well, at least we have not had to spend time watering our yard."

- "Mrs. Stern is so strict." Your response: "Yes, she is strict. At least we have peace and quiet in the classroom when we are trying to work on our assignments."

- Always reply to someone's comment or question. If you do not know an answer, be honest and say, "I really do not know much about that," or "I have not yet decided how I feel about that."

- To avoid one word answers, ask questions that do not have yes or no for answers. Rather than, "Are you going out of town for the summer?", ask "What are your plans for the summer?" The person will then have to reply with more than one word. Use this effective technique when talking with a shy girl or boyfriend.

Compliment: The applause that refreshes.
John W. Wierlein

COMPLIMENTS IN CONVERSATION

Start a conversation by giving someone a sincere compliment. A compliment can make the other person feel relaxed and able to carry on a better conversation. Giving a compliment is the opposite of judging someone. A compliment can also make someone who is sad, happy again.

Make sure that your compliment is sincere and truthful. Do not tell someone you like her dress, if you do not. You could tell her that you like the color of her dress. An insincere compliment is called flattery. Flattery is telling someone what you think he wants to hear in order to win his favor. Flattery is not genuine and certainly not from the heart.

Clothes, accessories and hair are not the only things to be complimented. I have cheered up a tired sales person by complimenting her on her helpfulness.

Complimenting someone on her smile can give her encouragement to keep spreading sunshine. "Your lovely smile really brightens my day."
I have been complimented on the way that I carry myself. This has encouraged me to always be graceful and poised.

Complimenting a child for being well behaved in a restaurant or on an airplane will encourage him or her to be well-mannered again.

Mothers like to be complimented for cooking a delicious meal and fathers for fixing, say, a broken curling iron or hockey stick. Young people enjoy a kind word about how neat they keep their bedroom. We all like to receive compliments.

HOW DO I SOUND?

Now that you know how to start and carry on a conversation, you need to know how you sound to others. If you are too loud, you will sound harsh. If too soft, you will appear to be fearful of talking to others. Does your voice sound respectful when you speak to adults and others in authority? What about the "Ums," "You knows," and other repetitive phrases?

Pronounce words correctly and you will be more easily understood. Only a ventriloquist should talk through his teeth. To keep others from having to continually ask you to repeat a sentence, open your mouth and move your lips when you speak. Take the time to pronounce words and syllables carefully. This is called proper enunciation.

Reading over tongue twisters is a great way to help you with your enunciation. "She sells sea shells down by the sea shore." Can you read this tongue twister without stumbling over any of the words?

Should you correct someone for mispronouncing a word? Unless he or she is a family member, I would not. Ladies and gentlemen never desire to embarrass anyone. They also know not to correct an adult, even one of their parents or relatives.

Tape your voice to hear how you sound in a natural conversation. Tape your side of a conversation while talking on the telephone with a friend. With your family's permission, tape a family dinner conversation. When you play back the tape, you will get a good idea of the areas in which you need to work.

Practice the above conversational skills and you will gain confidence in speaking with friends of all ages as well as with new acquaintances. People will become relaxed around you because of your positive, clear speaking style. They will appreciate your ability to draw them into a conversation with your focus on "them" instead of on "you."

REVIEW
Conversations

1. Speak clearly. This is called good _____.

2. Make eye contact! This reflects a good listener.

3. List three conversation starters. You may name your own or use some of the ones in the book.

        a)

        b)

        c)

4. Why shouldn't you whisper in a conversation?

_____

5. To avoid one-word answers, ask questions that do not have _____ or _____ for answers.

6. Think of someone (w/o mentioning any names) with whom you have had difficulty in carrying on a conversation. Why was this conversation difficult?

_____

7. When you compliment someone in a conversation, your compliment should always be _____ and _____.

Dear Parent,

Give your son or daughter opportunities to practice effective communication skills. Designate him/her to become the host or hostess at one of your family meals, having the responsibility for guiding positive and flowing conversation. Coming to the table with a list of some of the conversation starters in this chapter will eliminate frustration for a lack of something to talk about.

When I started dating, my mother and I rehearsed possible topics of conversation to discuss with my date. Building confidence by role playing helped me to relax and focus on making my date feel more at ease.

When your son or daughter learns how to "keep the ball rolling" in a conversation, he will feel less intimidated and more eager to talk with a variety of people on a diversity of subjects.

Deborah Wuerslin

LIFE LINE
Implementing Excellence

Telephone Manners

May the words of my mouth and the meditation of my heart be pleasing in
your sight,
O Lord.
-Psalm 19:14

"Reach out and touch someone," says, AT&T commercials. Although you can't physically touch someone through the phone, AT&T knows you can touch someone's emotions. You can brighten someone's day by sharing kindness over the phone. You can be helpful, comforting, loving, ...

Telephone skills do not always come naturally. Businesses spend thousands of dollars training employees to cultivate phone communication skills. Clear, concise, and courteous information helps build personal self-confidence and meaningful relationships with others.

Pleasant words are as honeycomb, sweet to the soul, and healing to the bones.

TELEPHONE MANNERS

Since the person you are call cannot see you over the telephone (until we all have picture phones), the receiver judges you solely by your voice. If you sound cheery, people will think you are friendly. If you just mumble when you answer, people might think that you are not very smart.

Did you know that a businessman will often judge a company by the way a secretary answers the telephone? When you answer your phone, you represent your entire family.

Think of the telephone as another opportunity to make people happy. Be polite. Never be rude. If someone calls and is rude or says bad things, do not say anything. Simply hang up.

DIALING. When you place a call, take the time to dial correctly. It is a good idea to have the number written down in front of you.

WRONG NUMBER. Do you slam the phone down fast? Never! Be polite and say, "Oh, I am sorry. I have the wrong number. Good Bye." You may also say, "I am sorry I disturbed you. Good bye."

IDENTIFY YOURSELF. As soon as someone answers, immediately say, "Hello, this is Debbie Smith. May I please speak to Suzanne Wiley?" Always identify yourself, even if the person who answers knows you. Never just say, "Is Suzanne there?"

DON'T PASS ME BY. If you recognize the voice on the other end, take a few seconds to say hello. To be polite say, "Hello Mrs. Myers. This is Mike Devaney. How are you today?" ("Fine, thank you.") "May I please speak to Kenny?" Adults, as well as young people, like to be recognized and not passed by. Please take the time to say hello.

NOT AT HOME. If the person you want to speak to is not at home, please leave a message. If you do not want your call returned, at least say, "Please tell Janet that I called. Thank you. Good Bye."

ANSWERING MACHINES. Please leave your name, the name of the person with whom you wish to speak, the date and time of your call, and a short message. Do not just hang up. The answering machine is meant for your convenience.

PLEASE AND THANK YOU. HELLO AND GOOD BYE. As in any conversation, always be polite.

LENGTHY CALLS. If you need to talk for a long time, AFTER you identify yourself, ask if this is a convenient time to call.

PRANK CALLS. Playing jokes on people, by pretending to be someone else, making weird noises, or saying bad things, is not only rude but is against the law.

BUSINESS CALLS. If a sales person allows you to use the store phone, make your call brief. Only use the store phone if it pertains to your purchase. Otherwise, use a pay phone.

DURING A CONVERSATION. Make sure that there is no background noise. If the television is too loud, do not shout, "Hey, turn down the t.v.!" Say to the person on the other end, "Just a moment please." Go in the other room and either turn down the television or politely ask that someone turn it down.

CHOMP. CHOMP. Eating while talking on the phone is impolite. A lady or gentleman would not do this.

WHEN ANSWERING THE TELEPHONE:

ANSWERING.
Ask your parents how they would like for you to answer the telephone. Either answer by saying a pleasant, "Hello," or answer with "Wuerslin residence. Paul speaking." Both ways are correct.

143

THAT'S NOT FUNNY.

I once heard someone answer the telephone, "Joe's pool hall. Eight ball speaking. What side pocket do you want to speak to." This is sort of cute, but this is no way to answer the telephone. What if the President was calling your father!

FOR YOU.

If you answer the telephone with "Hello" and the person who is calling asks to speak to you, do not say "Speaking" or "It is I." The correct way to respond is "Hello. This is Kirk."

NOT FOR YOU.

If the call is for someone else, please do not shout, "MARK, TELEPHONE!." Instead, say "Just a moment, please." Gently put the receiver down and go find Mark. If he cannot come to the phone right away, say to the caller, "Mark will be with you in just a moment." If you know Mark's friend, you could say a few kind words.

NOT AT HOME.

If the call is for someone not at home, say "Laura is not at home right now. May I please take a message?" Your parents may want you to say, "My parents cannot come to the phone right now. May I take a message?"

MESSAGES.

Have a family meeting and agree on where to put phone messages. Do not try to remember a message or number by heart. Get paper and pencil.

AN ADULT FOR AN ADULT.

If the adult caller does not identify himself, as would a young person, do not ask who is calling. Some adults resent having to identify themselves to a young person.

WRONG NUMBER.

If the caller appears to have the wrong number, ask "What number are you dialing?" If that is not your number, say "I am sorry, you have the wrong number. Never give the caller your telephone number.

INFORMATION PLEASE.

If someone calls and asks you a lot of questions, say "Just a moment please" and go get one of your parents. Never give out information over the phone, even if the person says you have won a big prize and they need to get your name, address, and other information. I always tell them that I do not give out information over the telephone.

A FRIEND'S PHONE.

When you are at a friend's house, always ask permission to use his telephone rather than just picking it up and dialing. Do not answer his telephone for him, either, unless asked to do so.

EAVESDROPPING.

Do not listen in on someone else's conversation. Give her the same privacy you would expect from her.

ON THE JOB.

Do not make personal calls while baby-sitting or working.

AFTER HOURS.

Do not make calls after 10:00 p.m. In our home, our children are to be off the telephone by 9:30 p.m.

GIRLS CALLING BOYS.

Sorry. You will have to wait for your dreamboat to call you. Although a few young men enjoy girls calling them, most find these girls aggressive and their calling annoying.

Call a boy only if you have a question about schoolwork, you are returning his call, or are inviting him over to your house. Of course, you need to call him if you have to cancel a date.

Conclusion

The telephone provides an easy and valuable method for talking to people far away. Treat the telephone with respect by using it properly and you'll earn the respect of those with whom you speak.

REVIEW
Telephone Manners

1. Answer the telephone every chance you get. Practice your new telephone skills, remembering to put a smile in your voice.

2. _____ Ask your parents how they want you to answer the telephone -- "Hello" or "Wuerslins" (using your own last name) or "Wuerslin residence. Diane speaking."

3. If the call is for someone else, how do you call the right person to the phone?

_____

4. When one of your friend's parents answers the phone, what is something you could say before asking to speak to your friend? _____

_____

5. Where should you put phone messages?

_____

6. Should you quickly hang up when you discover you have dialed a wrong number? Yes or No.

7. _____ Tape a telephone conversation (your voice only). Play back later and listen for speech ticks.

Telephone Manners

Dear Parent,

After reading this chapter with your son or daughter, discuss how you would like him to answer the telephone. Keep a pad and pencil near every phone and determine where to put written phone messages.

Practice proper telephone manners through role playing. Reinforce these manners by complimenting your son or daughter when he even attempts to answer the telephone in a clear and positive manner. "Ryan, thank you for answering the telephone so politely." "Heidi, Mrs. Keheeley said she appreciated your interest in her new job when you called to speak with Laurie the other day."

Positive encouragement reaps positive results.

Deborah Wuerslin

LIFE LINE
Implementing Excellence

Entertaining
Invitations, Party Time, Being a Good Host/Hostess, A Gracious House Guest, Thank-you Notes

For I know the plans I have for you," declares the Lord, "plans to prosper you and not to harm you, plans to give you hope and a future."
Jeremiah 29:11 NIV

Any enterprise is built by wise planning, becomes strong through common sense, and profits wonderfully by keeping abreast of the facts.
Proverbs *24:3,4* Living

Entertaining, when thoughtfully planned, brings smiles to your guests and satisfaction to you. Your guests can experience God's comfort, joy, and peace in your home when you are relaxed because you've taken the time to plan ahead, thinking of your guests' needs first. With enough practice, you'll even be able to entertain on the spur of the moment without becoming a nervous wreck.

Plan a party on your own, and you are totally on your own. Include the Lord in your plans, and he will guide your preparations. Creativity will flow more easily. You will be more sensitive to the needs and preferences of your friends. If you do make a mistake, God will give you the grace to carry on.

When plans become complicated and frustrating, pray again. Focus on the fun time your guests will enjoy in your home rather than the drudgery of the plans and work involved. *Cheerfully share your home with those who need a meal or a place to stay for the night.* 1 Peter 4:9 Living Bible

Make every guest feel special. *Let us stop just _saying_ we love people; let us _really_ love them, and _show it_ by our _actions._* 1 John 3:18 Living Bible. As a guest, "*be gentle and courteous to all.*" Titus 3:2b Living Bible. Recognize and show kindness to every family member of your friend's when visiting his home. Show appreciation for hospitality by sharing kind words and offering to help with chores. Send a thank-you note following a party or extended visit as a house guest. Concentrate on how you can share God's love, rather than thinking about what others are giving to you.

A man, sir, should keep his friendships in constant repair.
-Dr. Samuel Johnson

INVITATIONS

Invitations play an important role in our social life. They are an expression of our graciousness and thoughtfulness.

Invitations can be extended in person, by telephone, or written. A verbal invitation, however, can be easily forgotten. If you want to ask your mother if a friend can spend the night, do not ask in front of your friend. This puts your mother in an awkward position if she has to say no, as well as embarrassing your friend. The rule in our house is, if you ask in front of your friend, the answer is "No." Talking to your parents in private saves all involved from embarrassment.

Don't let this rule discourage you from being sharing, spontaneous, or hospitable. In certain situations where a friend would feel rejected, I might make allowances for being a gracious host. However, a long private talk about asking in front of a friend, with clear guidelines and warning about specific consequences, would be sure to follow.

Whether your invitations are formal or informal, you want them to give the desired impression. Design your invitation to convey a message of warmth and clarity.

FORMAL INVITATIONS are engraved or handwritten on conservative paper, nothing flashy. They are sent three to four weeks in advance for such occasions as weddings, graduations, formal dinners or dances, debuts, or official functions. An R.S.V.P. card is included along with a self-addressed, stamped envelope.

INFORMAL INVITATIONS, the type that a young person most often uses, are for birthday parties, slumber parties, dinner parties, luncheons, and teas. An informal invitation may be extended by telephone, handwritten on folded paper, filled out on pre-printed invitations, or designed on your computer, or prepared by a professional printer.

Although writing out invitations takes more time, your friends will have all the necessary information before them. Oral invitations can become easily forgotten and details mixed up.

Send your invitations out about two weeks before the event. Your friends will need enough notice to set this special date aside on their calendar, as well as make any special arrangements, (transportation, costume...) if necessary. Guests incline to forget invitations sent out too far in advance.

All invitations should include:

WHO:	Your name (first and last)
WHY:	The occasion
WHEN:	The date (day, month and date)
	The time (beginning and ending)
WHERE:	Location (include a small map, when necessary)
WHAT TO WEAR:	Dressy, casual, or play (shorts or jeans), costume
WHAT TO BRING:	Tennis racket, swim suit & towel, sleeping bag and pillow...
R.S.V.P.	Your phone number and full address

Receiving invitations is exciting. To inform your hostess you are looking forward to attending (or regretful that you cannot attend), always respond. R.S.V.P. is a French word for "Repondez, s'il vous plait" and means "Respond, if you please." You may R.S.V.P. by phone if there is a phone number next to the R.S.V.P. If a response card is included, as in a formal invitation, fill it out and put it in the mail. R.S.V.P. in the same manner the invitation is given. If the invitation is formal, the response should be formal.

Asking whom the other guests are before you give your reply is impolite. Your hostess will think her guests are more important to you than her party. After you reply, you may, however, ask if there is anyone your hostess has invited who lives near you so you can work out a carpool. Parents always appreciate this thoughtful question.

Why is an R.S.V.P. important? People cannot plan a party adequately if they don't know how many are attending. They need to know how much food to prepare, how many dishes they need, how much space they need, how many chairs, how many party favors, and what type of entertainment to plan. If you plan a dinner party and someone cannot come, you would like to know so that you can invite someone in their place.

Let's say that you had planned a party of fifteen and only five people responded to the invitation. You assumed that no one else was coming. The day of the party, all fifteen guests showed up! You were so embarrassed because you did not have enough refreshments or chairs set out.

Here is a sad, true story. One of my sons wanted to have a birthday party. My husband and I were so proud of him because he designed and printed all of his invitations, using our computer. His party was to treat his soccer team to a game of putt-putt golf and then to take them to a local park for a picnic and games. Only three boys out of twelve responded. One of the three said he could only make it to the picnic. Two teammates showed up at the putt-putt course at the correct starting time. After waiting 30 minutes while Paul and his guests played video games, we told Paul that he needed to start the party with his guests. He looked so disappointed. My husband and I told him that he had the responsibility of showing his two guests a good time, that they should not have to suffer for the other boys lack of consideration in responding. How would you have felt?

A friend of mine was given a baby shower years ago. No one responded to the invitation, so the woman giving the shower, assumed everyone was coming. Not one person showed up! How do you think my friend felt?

Please be a responsible person and always respond to an invitation *whether or not you plan to attend.* R.S.V.P. *within a few days.* If you said yes but cannot make the party at the last minute, please call and tell your hostess. When you do, others will look to you as a responsible and dependable young man or woman. Now that you know how to send an invitation as well as how to accept one, you can learn how to be a thoughtful host and gracious guest as well. You can learn how to give successful parties as well as enjoy the ones you attend.

When all looks gloomy, make a rainbow and watch the sun appear.
-Deborah Wuerslin

PARTY TIME!

What makes a successful party? Your party is a hit when each of your guests feels relaxed and able to mix and to talk with one another. A successful party has planned activities and a host who knows how to keep the conversation going so that no one gets bored. A successful party is fun! No one will want to leave and everyone will want to come back.

Having the right attitude and good planning are the keys to a successful party.

BE POSITIVE

Be positive and know that you can have a successful party. Rather than moaning about your house being too small for a big party, invite a small group of friends. If you want a lot of friends, have a buffet dinner instead of a sit-down dinner. Not enough chairs? Use the floor to sit on and make the dress casual. Move outdoors and have a barbecue.

> One year my daughter's outdoor birthday party was rained out. Rather than crying about the weather, Diane and I had her little guests sit on plastic tablecloths on the kitchen floor. Diane hosted an indoor picnic and everybody giggled and had fun. Rather than focusing on the bad weather, Diane and I looked at the bright side of things. We turned rain into sunshine. We made a rainbow!

Another excuse for being afraid to have a party is that no one will have a good time; everyone will just sit there. Make a rainbow! Plan your party so no one will have time to yawn. If the conversation dies down, have a joke or trivia question on hand.

154

GOOD PLANNING

First decide on a budget -- how much money can you spend on your party. Then decide how many guests you can easily handle with the available space. Will you have your party in the dining room, living room, garage, backyard or some other place?

A small group of fewer than 12 guests communicates more easily than a large group of friends. Break up a large group of 20 or more into small groups. Arrange chairs in several different groupings rather than one large circle. Groups between 12 and 20 tend to be awkward and make conversation difficult.

Around *two weeks* before your party, decide on the date, time, theme, decorations, guests, activities, refreshments, and dress. Send out invitations.

ONE TO TWO WEEKS BEFORE THE PARTY:
____ Call guests who have not responded.
____ Purchase or make decorations.
____ Buy or order food.
____ Check on entertainment -- records, radio, live music.
____ Prepare games, if any.
____ Buy or make prizes, if any.

THE DAY BEFORE THE PARTY:
____ Clean house and guest bath.
____ Set the table or buffet table and gather all serving dishes.
____ Decorate.
____ Move furniture, if necessary.
____ Decide where to place presents.
____ Decide where to place guests' coats.
____ Make up a party schedule for activities, refreshments and presents.

You will need to allow about 20 minutes if serving cake and ice cream, 30 minutes for eating lunch and at least 45 minutes for dinner.

155

DAY OF THE PARTY:

___ Give yourself plenty of time to get ready so that you have time to relax before your guests arrive.

___ Purchase cake, if ordered.

___ Remove any breakable items that you would hate to see broken.

___ Set out game items.

___ Get music ready.

AT THE PARTY:

• Ask for a friend or parent to take guests' coats and presents. Have a preplanned place for each.

• Make sure that you introduce your guests to one another.

• Start an activity right away to prevent your guests from becoming bored.

• Have a friend or parent record the presents. Thank you notes are thoughtful even though you will thank each guest in person.

• Show equal pleasure when opening gifts. Remember, it is the thought that counts. Say, "Thank you, _____," using the person's name.

• Although you want to have fun, too, always keep an eye out for the needs of your guests. They come first.

• Spend time with every guest.

• Offer refreshments to your guests before eating them yourself.

• Begin wrapping up the party near the prearranged time for the party to end. Looking at your watch, comment that the fun time has passed so quickly.

• When the party is supposed to be over, you might have to give a hint by asking your parents to appear. You may also start to pick up.

- When the party is over, walk each guest to the door and thank them for coming.

- Clean up.

- Show appreciation to anyone who helped you with the party. Did you know that parents treasure thank-you notes?

PARTY GUEST

- Remember to R.S.V.P.

- Select a gift with the receiver in mind, not just a gift you would enjoy.

- Shake hands when meeting someone.

- Offer to help serve and clean up, but don't insist if you receive a polite, "No, thank you."

- If you are the guest at a party, leave at the scheduled time.

- Unless you must, never leave a party before the guest of honor. This rule applies to weddings, as well. The bride and groom should be the first ones to leave. What if everyone left early and there was no one whom to catch the bride's bouquet?

- Always thank your friend before you leave. Thank his or her parents, too!

For manners are not idle, but the fruit of loyal nature and of noble mind.
-Alfred Lord Tennyson

BEING A GOOD HOST AND HOSTESS

The thoughtful, successful host and hostess create a comfortable and pleasant atmosphere for their guests. They make their goal that all guests become involved. Their key to success is through careful planning and a desire to give to others.

Having a party or an overnight guest? Check with your parents first. If you get the green light, plan your activities and food. Read the section on "Entertaining" to show you the way. Your guests will feel special when they know you have taken the time to make their visit an enjoyable one.

PREPARE AHEAD
Don't be running around once your guests have arrived. You want to be calm and enjoy every minute with them. Aim at being ready at least four hours before the party begins. Get plenty of rest.

When you invite your friends, give them all of the necessary details: date, time, address, what to wear, and what to bring. If you have planned an activity that involves money, let your friends know whether or not you will cover the expenses. Be a thoughtful host/hostess and ask them about any food preferences or allergies.

GUEST ROOM
Someday you might have a special room for house guests. Even if you do not, the following list includes little niceties to make your guests more relaxed.

- Clean sheets on bed.
- Extra blanket nearby.
- Chair, stool or bench to hold an open suitcase. A folding camp stool works well and can be stored away. A suitcase can ruin a bedspread. Who wants to open a suitcase on the floor?

- Clean towels and wash cloths. Show your guests where to hang them.
- Drinking cup in the bathroom.
- An extra new toothbrush. Many guests often forget to bring their own.
- A mirror.
- A night light to prevent your guest from stumbling around in the dark in an unfamiliar setting.
- Chair. Now your guest will not have to sit on the bed.

On the bedside table:

- A glass and container for water. Guests often find it difficult to move around in the dark in an unfamiliar house.
- Reading light.
- Alarm clock.
- Couple of magazines.
- Box of tissues.
- Vase with fresh flowers is the perfect touch.

Will a friend be sharing your room? Make sure that your bed has clean sheets and your room and bathroom are neat and clean. Show your guest where to store his or her belongings. A cleaned out drawer for your guest to use would be thoughtful.

GUEST ARRIVAL

- Introduce your guests to your parents. Do not leave out your brothers and sisters.

- Explain your family rules at appropriate times. Examples such as, keeping food in the kitchen area and leaving muddy shoes at the door.

- Show your guests where to hang their coats and place any other belongings.

- Be flexible with your planned activities. Give your guests a choice or let them think of an activity. Have some ideas so you do not waste all of your time asking one another, "What do you want to do?" "I don't know. What do you want to do?"

- You and your guests should clean up after your activities.

- Don't spend time talking on the telephone. Devote your time to your guests.

- Always speak highly of your family. Keep family arguments and secrets to yourself.

- Include all guests in activities and conversations.

- The host/hostess has the responsibility to steer any negative conversation into a positive one.

- Keep a sense of humor when disaster strikes. The host/hostess should be the first one to laugh.

> My friend could have cried when she discovered that she had forgotten to turn on the oven. Her beautiful roast was still raw when she was ready to serve dinner to her guests. Rather than making a fuss, she laughed. Her guests laughed with their hostess. My friend called and ordered the main course delivered. The fried chicken tasted better than usual with the hostess' potato casserole, tossed salad and chocolate cheesecake. Her guests applauded her for saving the dinner. They admired her for being a good sport about her crisis.

GUEST DEPARTURE

- When your friends have to leave, help them gather their belongings.

- Walk your guests to the door. This includes a friend who just came over for a short visit.

- Make your guests at ease in their surroundings. Be kind and thoughtful and they will be glad they came.

Fine manners need the support of fine manners in others.
-Ralph Waldo Emerson

BEING A GRACIOUS HOUSE GUEST

A gracious house guest appreciates any hospitality. A guest shows respect to his or her friend and family. The guest's speech and actions reflect a thoughtful and pleasant attitude. He or she thinks, "How can I help my friend to relax and enjoy our visit together?" "How can I pitch in and help?" "Am I showing gratitude for the time and effort made to make my stay a pleasant one?"

Start off on the right foot by promptly responding to an invitation. Do not be one of the guests your host has to call to find out if you will be attending the party or spending the night.

- Ask arrival and departure times. Some guests forget to ask when they are expected to leave. They overstay their welcome.

- Ask what type of clothes to bring.

- Ask about bringing a pillow, sleeping bag, games, records, sports equipment, ...

- Make a checklist of everything you will need to take with you. A thoughtful guest does not constantly borrow forgotten items from his or her friend.

- If you accept an invitation, do not change your mind for "a better offer."

- If you accept an invitation and agree to bring some food or other items, such as paper products, drop by the promised food or items

161

even if you have to cancel out. Do not make your hostess have to make last minute changes.

- Never bring an uninvited guest. If you have an out-of-town guest visiting you, call your hostess. Ask her if you can bring your visiting friend or relative.

ARRIVAL

The first time you spend the night or whenever you attend a party, take a hostess gift for the family. Homemade cookies or flowers are always appreciated. If the family plays tennis, a can of balls makes a cute gift. Keep the gift simple. The thought is what counts.

- Arrive on time, but never early.

- When you arrive, make sure that you meet and greet your friend's parents.

- Be friendly to all of your friend's family members. Call them by name.

- Learn any family rules.

- Ask your friend where to keep your belongings. Keep them in that one place rather than scattered all around the house.

BE A PLEASANT GUEST
- A gentleman and a young woman of confidence always remember their please and thank-you's.

- Be on time for meals and activities.

- Volunteer to help your friend. You can have fun performing simple chores, such as dishes, together.

- Make your bed.

- Do not place any dishes or food on any unprotected furniture. Ask your friend where to place them.

- Pick up after yourself.

- Always ask to use the telephone. Make your call as brief as possible.

- Don't play detective and spy through drawers, rooms, or someone else's mail.

- Don't help yourself to someone else's perfume, cologne, or beauty and hair products.

- Raiding the food pantry or refrigerator is rude. Wait until something is offered to you.

- Did you witness a family argument or learn of a family secret? Shhhh! Respect another family's privacy and keep this information to yourself.

- How embarrassing to break something! Everyone has accidents. Be honest. Tell your hostess. Offer to get it repaired or replaced.

- Ask permission to change the station on a radio. Your taste in music could offend your host or his family.

- Please use proper table manners.

- Do you remember how a gentleman and young woman of confidence sit in a chair? Sink gently rather than plopping down.

- Compliment your host and hostess.

THANK-YOU NOTES

Show appreciation for hospitality by sending a thank-you note within three days of your return home. Expressing gratitude strengthens relationships. A polite and thankful guest will be invited again.

Write your thank-you note in ink and be specific about what you enjoyed. A younger child may send a picture with a signature.

SAMPLES:

DINNER

Dear Mrs. Bricker,

The dinner at your house last Saturday was a meal to remember. I already thanked Allison for inviting me, but I wanted to drop this special note to you.

You must be one of the best cooks around. The pepper steak was so tasty and tender. I had to restrain myself from eating that second slice of chocolate cheesecake you offered to me, only because I am watching my weight. Yummy!

You have a way of making me feel a part of your family. I feel so relaxed and happy when I visit your home. Thank you for a wonderful evening.

Sincerely,

PARTY

Dear Chris,

What a blast! Your party was so much fun. I am so glad you invited me.

You sure spent a great deal of time planning for your "Sixties" Party. Usually I feel shy at parties around girls. Your games and activities, however, kept me laughing and made socializing a breeze. I especially liked the pantomime game.

Thank your mom for the great food.

Your friend,

WEEK END

Dear Judy,

I will long remember my weekend with your family. How thoughtful of you for including me in your Fourth of July celebration in the mountains.

Your parents treated me as one of the family by joking with me and even having me participate in camp chores. (My parents still don't believe I cleaned my own fish.)

Sharing your two-man tent and chatting through the night gave me the opportunity to get to know you better. I sure am glad we are friends.

Thank you for inviting me to share in this fun trip.   I had often dreamed of camping and hiking. You've got me hooked!

Love ya,

REVIEW
Entertaining

1. How long should you take before you respond to an R.S.V.P.? (Invitations)

_____

2. Why is an R.S.V.P. important? ("Invitations")

_____

3. How far in advance should you plan your party? ("Party Time!")

_____

4. What two things can you do the day before the party? ("Party Time!")
    a)
    b)

5. When the party is over, should you:
    a) Pick up as your guests leave?
    b) Walk each guest to the door and thank them for coming?

6. What two things can you put in the Guest Room to make your company more comfortable? ("Being A Good Host and Hostess")
    a)
    b)

7. You should introduce your guests to _____
("Being A Good Host and Hostess: Guest Arrival").

8. Before they arrive, gracious guests ask about arrival <u>and</u> _____
times. ("Being A Gracious House guest")

9. If you agree to bring food (or other items) to a party and cancel out at the last minute, do you still have to drop by the food? ("Being A Gracious House guest")   Yes or No

10. Should a guest be able to change the radio station at someone's house? Yes or No

Dear Parent,

"If you tell me I may listen; if you show me I may understand; if you involve me I will learn." (Unknown)

Planning and executing a party can mean the difference between chaos and an enjoyable event for all participants. Assist your son or daughter in planning a social event, such as a birthday party or pool party. Share in the excitement in planning and making preparations, eliciting his suggestions. When you serve more as the supporter rather than the planner, his confidence will grow as you place value on his ideas.

Ask your son or daughter which parties he/she has enjoyed attending in the past and why he/she considered them successes. Why did he feel comfortable spending the night in someone else's home? Without pointing the finger at anyone in particular, talk about unpleasant party experiences and visits in other's homes so he does not repeat these mistakes.

Together, read through the section on, "Being a Good Host and Hostess," and "Being a Gracious Houseguest." Your son or daughter may see how he has already applied some of the guidelines as a party host. "I remembered to show my guests where to hang their coats so they didn't toss them on the floor." "Becky was sitting quietly in a corner at my party, so I asked Caren and Laura to go over and talk with her." "David was such a thoughtful houseguest. He had kind words to say to my brother and sister and wrote a thank-you note to my parents as well as one to me."

Applying real-life situations to the guidelines in this chapter, makes these "rules" seem more logical and attainable.

Happy Entertaining!

Deborah Wuerslin

LIFE LINE
Implementing Excellence

Sincerely Yours

Give thanks in all circumstances.
1 Thessalonians 5:18 NIV

He guides the humble in what is right and teaches them his way.
Psalm 25:9 NIV

As a Christian, you represent Christ in all you say. Before corresponding with anyone, ask God for guidance. He will prepare your heart and mind. *But the wisdom that comes from heaven is first of all pure; then peace-loving, considerate, submissive, full of mercy and good fruit, impartial and sincere.* James 3;17 NIV

God desires for his children to fill their hearts with gratitude. Show your gratitude by saying "thank you", either verbally or through a thank-you note. Thank people for gifts, special favors, a lovely meal, a special date, for comforting you, or just for being a special person. What a wonderful way to share God's love.

Express sincerity and humility when writing a letter of apology. A letter of complaint will effectively communicate to its reader if your letter begins with a positive statement. Use Paul's letters to the church for examples of persuasive writing.

May your desire be, in all your writings, to let God's light shine.

The habit of expressing appreciation is oil on troubled waters. It is the essence of graciousness, kindness, and fair dealing. Fortunately, it is a habit that can be formed by anyone who will take the trouble.
-unknown

SINCERELY YOURS

Letters are so much fun to receive in the mail. They are like little visits from friends. They are conversations on paper.

This section will be dealing with informal correspondence, letters to friends and family.

STATIONERY

THE PAPER AND ENVELOPES
The paper and envelopes you choose for your correspondence, reflect your personality as much as the contents of your letters. You might like to use bright colors, pastels, or basic white. Ladies, your stationery may have flowers bordering each sheet, or your note cards with cute pictures on the front. Gentlemen, a border reflecting your hobby or favorite sport makes a smart choice. Some masculine colors for stationery are navy, burgundy, ecru, brown, and subtle shades of each.

As you grow older, you will want to use less ornate stationery. Good quality paper is more important than trying to use stationery that is too bold in color and design or cut in an unusual shape.

Some people prefer stationery engraved with their monogram or name and, perhaps, address. Envelopes may be plain or printed with the address. Coordinating the accent color of your stationery with the same colored pen is a choice you might like to make.

Keep in mind your reason for writing your letter and make your letter clear. Are you writing to congratulate someone, offer sympathy, thank someone, extend an invitation, or just to chat?

GETTING STARTED

THE ENVELOPE
        Help the postman and address the envelope neatly. If your handwriting is impossible to read, print the address. Only type the envelope if you type the letter. Your address, written in the upper left corner, is called the return address. If for some reason the mailman cannot deliver your letter, he will have your address on the letter to know where to return it. Place the postage stamp in the upper right corner. Center the mailing address on the face of the envelope. Use the two-letter designation for the state. For formal correspondence, such as a wedding invitation, write out the full name of the state.

```
T. Balkcolm
2020 Saddle Ridge                              stamp
Orlando, FL 30202


                         Mr. Chris Veith
                         500 Soccer Lane
                         Omaha, NE  68005
```

ADDRESSING ENVELOPES TO CHILDREN
        A young lady is not addressed as Miss until she is thirteen. Until then, just use her name. A young man is addressed as Master or just by his name until he is thirteen. As a thirteen year old, he can now be addressed as Mr.

ADDRESSING ENVELOPES TO ADULTS
        To a married woman --------------------Mrs. George Tota
                                (Use husband's name)

        To a divorced woman -------------------Mrs. Jacquelyn Tota

        To an unmarried woman ---------------Miss Jacquelyn Tota

To a business woman --------------------Ms. Jacquelyn Tota

Uncertain of marital status -------------Ms. Jacquelyn Tota

INK
Write in ink since pencil is harder to read and smudges easily. Business letters look more professional when they are typed, but always write your signature in ink. Use black ink for business but any color will do for an informal letter.

THE HEADING
Write the heading, your address and the date, at the top right-hand side. If writing to someone who knows your address, you only need to write the date.

THE INSIDE ADDRESS
The inside address consists of the name and address of the person to whom you are writing. Written above the salutation on the left side, the inside address is customary in business not in a letter to a friend.

Begin your letter with "Dear _____." This is the salutation or greeting. Use the same name that you use in conversation, "Dear Robin," or "Dear Uncle Michael." Write the salutation two lines below the date but next to the left margin or two lines below the inside address.

```
                                        112 Platte Place
                                        Denver CO 80843
                                        June 12, 1999
Ms. Iris Whitaker
333 West Park Place
New York, New York   00231

Dear Iris,
     XXXXX XX X XX XX  XX   XXXXXXX X XXX XXX  XXX
X XXX XX X XXXXXX XXXXX XXXX.  XX XXXX XXX XXX
XX.XXX XXX XXXXX XXXX.  XX XXXXX XXX XX XXXX XX.
```

THE BODY OF THE LETTER

Be natural when you write an informal letter to a friend or relative. Write as though you were talking to them. Share your activities and any information about anyone they know -- all kind words, of course. You can talk about a fun book you have just read or how you feel about a current event or activity in which you are involved. The list of conversation starters will give you more ideas.

Make sure you show interest in the person you are writing to. Your letter should not be filled with "I's." Ask questions about the person without grouping them all in one paragraph. "How are you? How is your summer? Is the weather nice? Are you swimming in your new pool?"

A better approach would be to ask, "Now that you have a pool in your backyard, are you able to swim laps every day to keep in shape for the upcoming soccer season?"

Neatness and appearance show the person you are writing to you care enough to write a letter that is both pleasing to read and easy to read. Your margins should be even on both sides and the stationery folded neatly.

Another courtesy to your reader is to number your pages. If the pages get mixed up, the reader can easily put them back in the correct order.

Strive for accuracy in mechanical details, spelling, dates, statements, grammar, and punctuation.

Clarity means communicating effectively. Make sure the reader understands what you are trying to say. Don't ramble on without expressing a definite idea.

Thoroughness. Review your letter, making sure you included all the desired information. When responding to someone's letter, answer all questions, or the recipient will be forced to ask you again.

When writing to a relative or close friend, you may end your letter with "Love," or "Affectionately." This is the complimentary close. "Sincerely," "Cordially yours," or "Yours truly," are a little more formal. Only capitalize the first word.

SIGNATURE
Your signature should always be handwritten. If the reader does not know you very well, use your first and last name.

THE POSTSCRIPT
Some writers like to use a P.S. at the end of their letter to make sure the reader remembers a certain point. The postscript starts at the left margin, two lines below the signature. Begin the message immediately after the P.S. Keep the message short. If the message extends one line, indent the second line where the message began.

P.S. Remember to call Uncle Dave and Aunt Candy when you vacation in Seattle. They can tell you where all of the best hiking trails are in the area.

TYPES OF LETTERS

LETTER OF INTRODUCTION

This letter is written to introduce someone you know to someone else. Someday you might ask a good friend, former boss, teacher or pastor to send a letter of introduction to a company where you desire an interview.

LETTER OF COMPLAINT

Perhaps you have to write to a company about a defective product or to a store about a rude employee. Think of something complementary to say at the beginning of your letter. This positive comment shows you are not a negative person. Keep your letter polite and simple. Stick to the facts.

LETTER OF APOLOGY

A letter apologizing for canceling a dinner date at the last minute or not attending a party would be a thoughtful gesture. You do not need to give any excuses. Just say something like, "I know I missed a wonderful time and hope I can get together with you soon." If you have a serious problem with someone, do not apologize in a letter but rather in person.

LETTER TO A PUBLIC OFFICIAL

You are never too young to write to a public official such as the President, a senator, governor or mayor. You are part of the government and need to express your feelings regarding current issues.

PERSONAL LETTERS

These are letters to friends and relatives. Follow the guidelines given above.

LETTER OF SYMPATHY

If you know someone who has lost a loved one or even a pet, a short note would be very thoughtful. Share how you feel. Try to share a fond memory about the person who just died. Offer to help in any way you can.

LETTER OF COMFORT

When you know someone who is sick, send a card to cheer him or her up. If you normally see that person on a regular basis, tell her you miss seeing her (or him). Cards can also be of great comfort when someone doesn't make a place on a team, a relationship breaks up, or somebody has to move away.

SPECIAL OCCASION CARDS

Printed cards for holidays such as Christmas, Easter, Valentines Day, Mother's Day, Father's Day, and birthdays, should always contain a personal note. Otherwise your card appears to be one of obligation.

THANK-YOU NOTES

This type of correspondence seems to be the most neglected yet is always received with enthusiasm. Everyone likes to be appreciated. A kind word encourages. No words of gratitude discourage.

If you thank someone in person for a gift, a thank-you note is not necessary but always appreciated by the giver.

Not only for gifts, but also write thank-you notes for: a hospital visit, a fun date, an enjoyable dinner party, for being an overnight guest, a job interview, someone who went out of their way for you .

Here are some guidelines for writing thank-you notes:

- Be prompt. Write your note within a week.

- Do not use printed notes. Write your own.

- Always write in ink. Typewriters or computers are not acceptable. Thank-you letters relating to a business may be typed on letterhead.

- Be friendly and sincere.

- Mention the gift, not just "Thank you for the gift."

- Share how you plan to use the gift and what makes it special.

- For money gifts, mention what you plan on doing with it (spend it on _____, savings, or investment).

- As a house guest, mention gratitude for any favors done, such as washing a muddy pair of sneakers or cooking a lovely meal.

Here are some sample thank-you notes to serve as guidelines:

OVERNIGHT GUEST

Dear U.R. Great,

Thank you so much for the wonderful time you gave me last weekend. (Then talk about the food, meeting friends, and any favors, such as laundry.)

Thank you again. It was so kind of you.

Your friend,

TYPICAL LETTER TO YOUNG MAN

Dear Romeo,

Thank you for a wonderful evening, which I enjoyed tremendously. It was so kind of you to take me to the Atlanta Ballet, which I thought was lovely.

Thank you, too, for the delicious dessert. I have such a weakness for chocolate.

Again, many, many thanks.

Yours affectionately,

GIFT

Dear Aunt Gem,

How did you know that I have always wanted a pair of pearl earrings? Now I have something special to wear on Easter Sunday with the pink dress Mom and Dad bought me.

Whenever I wear them, I will always think of you. You can be sure I will take special care of them.

Thank you again.

Love,

FAVOR

Dear Timothy,

Ever hear of an alarm clock? It's the thing that scares the daylight into you. Ha, ha, hee, hee.

I was scared I was going to miss out on my fishing trip with my dad because I broke my fishing pole the night before our trip. Thanks a lot for loaning your pole to me. I caught five big trout!

I hope you like the new tackle box. You trusted me to take care of your pole, so I bought you something to show my appreciation.

Your friend forever,

TEACHER

Dear Mrs. Nicetome,

My year with you has been the greatest. Although I found Geometry to be difficult, you gave me hope that I could conquer a difficult problem. You were patient and never laughed at my questions.

I pray that God will bless your future years as a teacher.

Thank you, again, for being such a wonderful teacher. I will always remember you.

Sincerely,

Take the time to write a thoughtful and sincere note. Remember that the best thank-you note is one that is personalized. You will gain a reputation for being a gracious and appreciative young lady or gentleman.

REVIEW
Sincerely Yours

1. May you write a letter in pencil?   Yes or No

2. Your signature should always be _____

3. What is the most effective way to write a letter of complaint?
_____

4. May you write a thank-you note on the computer?   Yes or No

5. To save time, may you use pre-printed thank-you notes?   Yes or No

6. Rather than just saying, "Thank you for the gift," you should
_____

7. Write thank-you notes within: a) one day, b) one week, c) when you get around to writing one.

8. ___ Write a thank-you note to someone, following the guidelines in this chapter.

Dear Parent,

Some young people jump right into the task of writing a thank-you note. They show creativity either through their words or a cute picture. The average young person, however, requires a gentle push and a lot of guidance.

Before my children could write, they drew pictures for their thank-you notes to relatives and friends. After they learned the alphabet, I wrote out simple letters for them to copy. As their confidence grew, they began composing their own letters with a few suggestions offered from me. Their grandparents motivated them to continue writing by sending my children individual letters of appreciation for their gratitude -- sort of a thank you for the thank you.

Not only for gifts, but your son or daughter can learn to write letters of appreciation to a teacher for extra time spent on explaining a difficult subject. He can thank a friend or neighbor for performing a special task. Her get-well cards and notes of cheer will bring smiles and comfort to the recipients.

Teach your son or daughter that letters are conversations on paper. Encourage them to write as though they were talking to the recipient of the letter in person. As in a conversation, the writer of a letter spends more time showing interest in whomever he is writing to, rather than writing endlessly about himself.

Thoughtful young people become thoughtful adults.

Deborah Wuerslin

LIFE LINE
Implementing Excellence

Dining Etiquette

Commit everything you do to the Lord. Trust him to help you do it and he will.
Psalm 37:5 Living Bible
Perseverance must finish its work so that you may be mature and complete, not lacking anything.
James 1:4 NIV

Dining etiquette rules can overwhelm you if you try to tackle everything at once. Just go one step at a time. As you master one skill, try another.

Pray for a teachable spirit, willing to receive guidance and even correction from your parents. Your manners will improve more rapidly if you put pride aside and remain teachable and humble.

Grab hold of determination. Determination will equip you with a hunger for learning. Studying this book won't satisfy you. You will read other books on dining skills and listen to adults who can teach you these skills. Most of all, *observe* and learn from others who have discovered the graces of life.

Embrace perseverance. Perseverance enables you to continue learning despite frustrations, mistakes and the boring repetitions of practicing your dining skills.

Etiquette is the combination of attitude, interest, self-motivation, teachability, eagerness, gratefulness, and practice. Others are drawn to these friendship qualities and tasteful manners.

There is always a best way of doing everything, if it be to boil an egg.
Manners are the happy way of doing them.
-Emerson

DINING ETIQUETTE

TABLE SETTING FOR THE SIT-DOWN DINNER

All of us have felt embarrassed at one time or another because we did not know the correct manners for a particular situation. Which fork am I supposed to use? How do I let the waiter know that I am finished with my meal? What do I do when my friend has me over for dinner and she does not have catsup on the table?

When you lose your confidence because you do not know proper table manners your smile fades away and you suddenly become very quiet. Your meal is less enjoyable. When you feel uncomfortable, you can bet your dinner companion is ill at ease, too. Insecurity is not easily hidden and spreads rapidly.

Gain confidence at mealtime by learning proper dining manners. Your smile will reappear. You will become less self conscious and interact with others. Even if you forget a rule, you will not become upset. You will know that good table manners are really common sense. You will be able to "fake it," knowing that next time you will remember the proper form of etiquette. Becoming upset will only make those around you uncomfortable. When you eat naturally, because you have practiced at home, everyone at the table will enjoy their meal and have a friendly conversation.

Did you know that bosses often take someone out to lunch or dinner before they decide to hire him or her? If the person who wants the job has poor table manners, he probably will not get the job. The employer might think he would embarrass other people in the office as well as clients. People with poor table manners also do not appear to be very smart.

People can laugh at babies for making funny noises while eating or for making a mess with their food. No one, however, laughs at an older noisy or messy eater.

Many, many years ago, people had no utensils. They ate with their fingers. Even then, however, etiquette dictated the proper way to eat. The person with no class dug into his food with all ten fingers. He wiped his gooey, greasy human utensils on a towel-like napkin or just licked the food off his hands.

People displaying good manners, usually those with a lot of money, knew that using hands like claws was not the correct way to eat. The proper way was to only dirty three fingers. The ring finger and pinky were stuck straight out to keep clean. Some people today think sticking out their pinky when sipping tea characterizes exquisite manners (Not so!).

Eating utensils also divided the classes of people (poor and rich). The spoon was invented to make eating soupy foods easier to eat. Poor people ate with carved wooden spoons and rich people had spoons made of silver and bronze. Only rich people had small table-size knives and they used forks long before people who could not afford them.

Americans were the first people to use a place setting, placing the knife, fork, and spoon on the table together. Each family took pride in how many different spoons, knives, and forks they could add to their individual place settings.

Today, during most meals, you will not have to use a multitude of silverware. If you ever do sit down to a table with lots of silverware, do not panic. Rather than being overwhelmed by the number of pieces, know that silverware is placed on the table according to which utensils you will need to use first. An easy rule to follow is to begin with the silverware on the outside of the place setting and work towards your plate with each course. For example, when you serve soup as the first course, place the soup spoon to the far right of the soup bowl on the outside of the other silverware.

PLACING YOUR SILVERWARE AND DISHES

The service plate, placed in the center, is larger than the dinner plate and goes under the plates for the appetizer, salad, and soup. When the main course (entree) is brought in, the service plate is removed. Usually you will only see a service plate in fancy restaurants.

The dinner plate is placed in the center of the place setting.

The salad plate is placed in the center if served before the entree and to the left of the forks if served with the entree.

Forks go to the left of the plate. Just remember that fork and left have four letters each so they go together. Knife and spoon each has five letters and so does RIGHT, so place them to the right of the dinner plate. Now you will never forget where to place the silverware.

The dinner fork is the large fork used for entrees and goes next to the dinner plate.

The salad fork, slightly smaller than the dinner fork goes to the far left or outside the dinner fork. When serving the salad after the entree, place the salad fork inside the dinner fork. *The salad fork is not necessary when serving the salad with the main course.*

The seafood fork is tiny with three tines and is used for an appetizer, such as a shrimp cocktail. Place this fork to the right of the spoons. If there are already three utensils on the right, place the seafood fork to the far left, outside the other forks. You may also bring this fork out with the appetizer.

Place the dinner knife just to the right of the dinner plate with the sharp edge of the blade towards the plate. In this way, you will not cut yourself if you accidentally pick it up by the blade.

The soup spoon, like the salad fork, is positioned according to when the soup is served. Generally, place the soup spoon to the right of the knife. Place it to the outside (right) of the teaspoon if you are to use the soup spoon before the teaspoon.

The teaspoon goes to the right of the knife.

Place the dessert fork and spoon above the dinner plate or bring them in with the dessert.

Proper Place Setting

The bread and butter plate goes above the forks.

The bread and butter knife is smaller than the dinner knife. It belongs horizontally at the top of the bread and butter plate, with the blade facing towards the center of the plate.

The water glass belongs slightly above the dinner knife.

The wine glass goes to the right of the water glass and slightly closer to you.

Place the cup and saucer to the right of the spoons.

The napkin is fun because you can place it almost anywhere, except under the table! You can place it to the left of the forks (not under), on top of an empty plate, in an empty glass, or above the plate. You can fold your napkin many different ways. You might enjoy using a pretty, funny or plain napkin ring. The napkin can come in any color, too.

During mealtime, the napkin rests on your lap. A small, luncheon napkin rests on your lap unfolded. Keep a large dinner napkin folded in half. The folded edge rests away from you. Now, when wipe your greasy fingers, you can pick up the top edge of your napkin and wipe them clean. The top part of the napkin will now rest on the bottom half of the napkin and not on your clothes.

Would you like a drink? Make sure that no food is left in your mouth before drinking. Blot your lips with your napkin before taking a drink so you do not smear your glass with food particles. Ladies and gentlemen don't desire to watch food floating around in their beverage or a greasy mess on their glass.

When leaving the table during a meal, say "Excuse me, please." Place your napkin to the left of your plate -- not on top of your food or on your chair. If you put your soiled napkin on your chair, you might sit on it when you return. You also take the chance of soiling a fabric-covered chair.

Try to leave the table only when necessary. Getting up and down like a yo-yo can be very disruptive to a meal.

When you complete your meal, place your napkin to the left, again. Never refold or crumple it. Always wait for your hostess to place her napkin on the table first. This is the hostess' signal that mealtime is over. A sharp hostess will make sure that everyone is finished.

MEALTIME MANNERS

GOOD GROOMING

Before meals, wash your hands and brush your hair. When someone has taken the time to make you a meal, even just a peanut butter and jelly sandwich, take the time to come to the table in a presentable manner. The sloppy look says that you do not care about others.

YOU MAY BE SEATED

In someone else's home, wait for the hostess to tell you when and where to be seated. Stand behind your chair until she sits down or tells you to be seated.

A Lady should allow a gentleman to seat her -- even at home. A gentleman pulls out a lady's chair. As she begins to sit down, he pushes the chair in. Sometimes she can help by raising up slightly so he can give the chair one last gentle push.

POSTURE PERFECT!

Please do not cross your legs under the table or fully stretch them out. You will probably kick someone. Don't wrap your feet around the chair legs nor rock back on the rear legs of the chair. Keep your feet flat on the floor or tucked under your chair.

Sit up tall. Elbows may only rest on the table between courses.

LEAN OVER

Lean over your plate when taking a bite without bending down. Keep your posture upright. Bring your utensil to your mouth rather than bending down to put it in your mouth.

GRACE

When at someone else's house, wait for the hostess to say grace. If you don't customarily pray, respect another's custom and bow your head. If your host does not say a blessing and you do, bow your head and say a silent, quick prayer without making a big show of your actions.

SERVING UTENSILS

The large serving spoon is used to cut and lift while the large fork holds the portion of food on top of the spoon. After serving yourself, place the serving fork and spoon side by side on the platter. Never use your utensils for serving. Ask your hostess if you need a serving utensil.

SERVING

Pass the food from left to right. Keep the salt and pepper shaker together, even when only one is requested. When passing a pitcher, turn the handle towards the person next to you so he or she can grab the handle.

Take only the amount of food you intend to eat.

Take the first piece of food you touch, rather than picking through everything first.

If you do not like something, take a small amount and then pass it on without saying a word. "Yuck, I don't like this" is rude behavior. Rather than dwelling on the negative, praise the positive. "Oh, I really like your potato casserole." Mothers need compliments occasionally, too.

If a dish does not get passed to you, ask for it. Never reach across the table. "Will you please pass the green beans?" "Thank you."

If you are in someone's home and you do not see something on the table that you normally like to use, do not ask for it. The hostess might become embarrassed that she does not have what you asked for. Maybe you like catsup on your scrambled eggs and you do not see any on the table. You will just have to eat your eggs without catsup this one time. If you are in a restaurant, you may ask the waiter for any condiment, such as catsup, mustard, salt & pepper, or other items which add flavor to your food.

When someone serves you, the server will stand at your left. Beverages *only* will be served from the right, so the server does not have to reach across you.

WHO EATS FIRST?

Your hostess will pick up her fork to signal the beginning of the meal or tell you, "Please start eating."

BASIC COURSES

SEAFOOD COURSE

The tiny fork at your place setting is for your seafood cocktail. If the bites are too big, use this fork to cut the seafood. Trying to use a knife in a tall dish would topple it over. When finished, place the fork on the plate under the cup.

SOUP'S ON!

Soup should be seen and not heard. Slurping or inhaling soup is not the way a lady or gentleman eats soup. Sip your soup quietly.

Steam rising from your soup or your bowl, hot to the touch, may indicate the soup is too hot to eat. Cooling down your soup by stirring, tossing, or blowing is not acceptable. The thought of adding ice cubes makes me shudder.

Skim your spoon across the top of the soup, the coolest part. Scoop away from you, with the far edge of the spoon picking up the soup. Sip a small tester bite from the edge closest to you or from the end of the spoon. In this way, no soup will dribble down your chin. If the small tester bite is piping hot, wait a couple of minutes. Enjoying conversation with friends for a short while gives your soup time to cool down.

For the last few bites, tilt the bowl away from you with your free hand. Now scoop the soup, still scooping away from you. If the soup bowl is on a plate, place the spoon on the plate when finished. Otherwise, leave the soup spoon in the empty bowl.

BREAD AND BUTTER
With the butter knife provided on the butter dish, take some butter and put it on the side of your bread and butter plate. If no plate is provided, put the butter on the edge of your dinner plate and the roll on the tablecloth.

Break a bite-size portion of roll and butter it with *your* butter knife. Do not butter the whole roll, only one bite at a time. The exception to this is with hot rolls, muffins, and toast. You may butter the entire portion while still hot.

As you break the roll and butter it, hold the roll over your butter plate rather than over your dinner plate. Your small butter knife rests along the top of your bread and butter plate when you are not using it.

Formal dinners do not serve bread, so there is no need for a bread and butter plate.

SALAD COURSE
You only need to place a salad fork on the table when serving the salad as a separate course. When you eat your salad with the main course, you may use your dinner fork. You may cut any large pieces with your knife.

MAIN COURSE (ENTREE)
When you were little, your mother or father cut up all of your food all at once. Now that you are older, you can cut your own meat.

Cut only two or three pieces of meat at a time. Cut small pieces so you can quickly answer a dinner companion's question. If he or she waits for you to chew a large piece, your companion forget the question. You might be tempted to talk with food in your mouth.

To cut your meat, put the dinner fork in your left hand with the prongs down, holding the meat in place. With the knife in the right hand and the fork (tines down) in the left, cut a small piece of meat. Keep the knife outside of the fork and not under it. Keep those elbows down! Besides looking like a flapping bird, you might elbow the person next to you.

After you cut one to three pieces of meat, rest the knife at the top of the plate. Keep the blade facing the center of the plate. Now put the fork in your right hand, tines up, and enjoy your food. This is called the zig-zag method and used most often by Americans.

The European or Continental method of eating has no switching. the fork remains in your left hand with the tines down with the knife remaining in the right hand.

Chew your food quietly. If your mouth remains closed, no one will hear you chomp or smack your lips.

Take small bites and chew your food thoroughly.

Please do not wave your fork around while talking. Set the fork down on your plate if you have something lengthy to share.

FINISHED POSITION
When you finish your meal, put your fork and knife side by side diagonally across the plate with the handles closest to you. The tines of the fork are up and the knife is to the right of the fork with the blade facing in. The waiter will take this as a signal to clear your dishes, and he will not have to ask you if you are finished.

> One year my church decided to hold their annual Christmas Banquet at a beautiful local hotel. At the end of our delicious meal, the waiter walked around my table asking everyone, "Excuse me. Are you finished?" When he finally came to me, he whispered "Thank you." My waiter did not have to ask me whether or not I had completed my meal. My utensils had been placed in the finished position. He knew that I had finished.

DESSERT COURSE
This is what you have been waiting for! To eat your delicious dessert, you may use both the fork and spoon provided or just one of them.

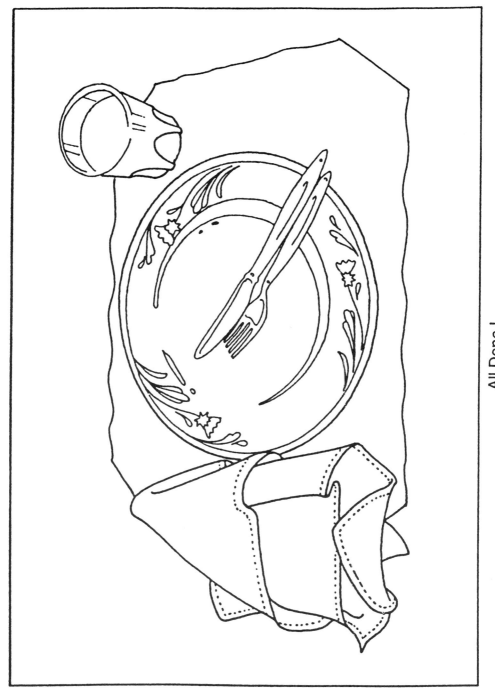

All Done !

(Eating with just one utensil is much easier.) If you use both, use the fork in the left hand to push the food onto the spoon. After eating the last bite, place the fork and spoon together on the plate below the dessert bowl. If the rim of the plate is too narrow, or the dessert dish does not come served on a plate, your utensisl may rest in the dessert bow.

FINGER BOWL

A finger bowl is sometimes used after eating messy foods such as corn on the cob or shellfish. To clean your hands, dip the fingers of one hand in the water in the finger bowl and then repeat with the other hand. Now dry your hands on your napkin.

If the finger bowl is served on a dessert plate with a fork and spoon, place the finger bowl with the doily under it to the left and above the center (where the bread and butter plate used to be). Place the dessert plate in the center with the fork on the left and the spoon on the right.

MORE TABLE MANNERS

TAKING FOOD OUT OF YOUR MOUTH

The way food goes in is the way it goes out. If you eat an olive with your fingers, take the pit out with your fingers (the index finger and thumb). If you eat steak with a fork (which I hope you do), then take the gristle, or any bit too difficult to chew, out of your mouth with your fork. Cover the partially chewed item with a piece of food so your dinner companions do not have to look at it.

ACCIDENTS

If you spill your drink, try to catch the liquid quickly with your napkin. If you spill on someone else, apologize and offer your napkin.

If you drop something on the floor, leave it there and ask for a replacement. In someone else's home, pick up the utensil yourself and ask for a replacement.

SNEEZING AND COUGHING

If you suddenly sneeze, cover your face with your napkin and turn your head. Then excuse yourself to go blow your nose in privacy with a kleenex or handkerchief. Never use your napkin, and never blow your nose at the table. When you return, have kleenex or a handkerchief within easy reach.

Turn your head away from your table companion when coughing and cover your mouth. If your cough persists, leave the table so as not to draw attention to yourself.

BURPING

In some foreign countries, a burp tells your host that you enjoyed your meal. A burp in the United States is definitely inappropriate.

BUGS AND HAIR

If you discover a bug or hair strand in your food, keep it to yourself. Remove the unwanted creature or hair and wipe it on your napkin. Please do not embarrass your hostess or make anyone else feel uncomfortable about your finding. Of course, in a restaurant, you may quietly ask your waiter for another bowl of soup when you discover a bug or hair.

ELBOWS

Elbows on the table ruin your posture, making you look sloppy, tired, or bored. *Only* place elbows on the table between courses (when not eating).

TOOTHPICKS

Only clean out food particles caught between your teeth in privacy. Using a toothpick or fingers is not appealing for someone else to watch. If you must, excuse yourself to the restroom and clear the food out. A purse-size toothbrush is so handy to carry along. Some men carry a plastic pocket-siz toothpick. Toothpaste is not necessary for their refreshing.

EVERYTHING IN!

Eat everything on your fork or spoon in one bite. If that is impossible, put less on your utensil.

TOO HOT!

If you take a bite of food that is too hot, don't spit it out. Drink some water. This is one time you can take a drink with food in your mouth.

To check for food that might be too hot, take a very small bite. Your mouth can usually handle a tiny piece of hot food. If the food is too hot to eat, enjoy a friendly conversation for a few minutes while your food cools down.

BREAD MOP

You may use bread to mop up gravy or meat juice. Stab a piece of bread with your fork and then mop up the gravy. Bread mopping with your fingers is not good manners.

FOOD WRAPPERS

Place food wrappers and packets in an ashtray, under the rim of the service plate or on your bread and butter plate.

CLEARING THE TABLE

When you are at someone's house, offer to help clear the table when the meal at the end of the meal. Do not insist if the answer is no. If you do clear, do not stack dishes.

As I was beginning to clear the table one evening during a dinner party, my guests had passed all the dishes to the end of the table while I was making my first trip to the kitchen. Should I have corrected my guests and told them that dishes should not be stacked? I did not, because my goal is never to make anyone to feel uncomfortable. Instead of even jokingly scolding them, I said, "Thank you" and carried the stack of dishes to the kitchen.

Always look at the intent or heart of people. If their intent is to be helpful, then be grateful.

Good manners apply to eating out as well as home. If you practice at home, eating out will seem less complicated and more enjoyable. don't worry about learning everything at once. Perhaps you can concentrate on one manner a day. I would rather you go slowly than not at all.

Have other family members read this book so you can practice together. What one of you forgets, the other will remember. Pick out one day a week where you can really concentrate on total dining etiquette.

> When I was growing up, my mother would make Sunday a special meal. She would set the table with linens, candles and her best dishes. One house in which we lived did not have a dining room table so my mother set up a table in the living room. We all felt special and tried extra hard to practice our mealtime manners. We checked our grooming, posture, eating habits and conversational skills. I have such pleasant memories of these special family meals.

At least for special occasions, ask your parents to take you out to a good restaurant. Our children select the restaurant of their choice (within our budget, of course) for their family birthday dinners. My husband and I do not allow them to choose fast-food restaurants for these special celebrations.

Speaking of fast food. Good manners belong in these restaurants, as well. Wear appropriate attire. Always be ready with your order when you go up to the counter. If an order is mixed up, be polite. No one trying to run a business is going to mess up an order on purpose.

Remain seated and talk quietly while you are eating. Did you wash your hands first? When you finish, clear the table and throw your trash out in the provided container.

SPECIFIC FOODS

Artichoke Leaves: Eat them with your fingers. Pull off one leaf and dip the base of it in the accompanying sauce. Then use your teeth to pull the tender part off the leaf. Discard the leaf in the bowl provided or on the side of your plate. After eating the edible leaves, cut the fuzzy inedible center away. Eat the "heart", using your fork and knife.

Asparagus: Although eating with fingers is acceptable, this long, limp vegetable is best eaten with a fork. Cut one bite at a time, using your dinner fork.

Bacon: Eat crisp bacon with fingers and fatty bacon with a fork.

Cake: Pound cake may be eaten with fingers, breaking off one bite at a time. Never put the whole piece up to your mouth. You may also eat a tiny piece of wedding cake with fingers. Eat moist cake, eclairs, and cream puffs with a fork.

Baked Potato: Slit the potato with your knife and squeeze it open with your fingers. Use your fork to add butter or sour cream. You may eat the skin, using your fork and knife.

Celery and Carrot Sticks: Finger foods.

Chicken: For informal meals, you may eat chicken with fingers. Learn how to cut chicken with a fork and knife. Eat meat served with a sauce with a fork.

You may pick up meat bones with one hand at an informal affair only after you have first used your fork and knife to strip off as much meat as possible.

Despite what the advertisers say, do not lick chicken from your fingers. Use your napkin.

Corn on the Cob: A finger food that is eaten only in informal dining. Butter only a few rows at a time, with your dinner knife, so the butter does not drip all over.

Crackers: You may break a few crackers at a time and float them on your soup.

Dips: Dip a raw vegetable, fruit, or chip in a dip or sauce only once. After you have taken a bite, never dip the same food again. What a wonderful way to spread germs.

Finger Foods: You may eat French fries and chicken nuggets with fingers. When served with the main course where you are using a fork, eat the French fries and nuggets with a fork.

Apples and Pears: Eat whole as a snack. At the table, cut in quarters and eat each quarter with your fingers or with a fork.

Bananas: At the table, peel and break off one bite at a time.

Grapefruit: Enjoy every last section, but don't squeeze the juice in your bowl or on your spoon and eat it.

Grapes: Cut off one cluster (or bunch), rather than pulling off one grape at a time. Put the cluster on your plate and eat one grape at a time.

Watermelon: You may hold the rind in two hands. Place the seeds into a cupped hand and onto your plate. You may also place the watermelon slice on your plate and remove the seeds with your fork.

Gravy: The gravy boat is not used to pour the gravy. Use the ladle and serve over the meat, potatoes or rice.

Ice cream, Custard, Puddings: Use a teaspoon. Remember, eat everything on the spoon in one bite.

Jams and Jellies: Place these on the dish beside the foods in which they will be eaten.

Parsley and other Garnishes: These greens are used for decorations. You may eat them with a fork.

Pizza: Finger food.

Tacos: Finger food. Eat from one end as you would do with toast or a sandwich.

Salt Cellar: Use the tiny spoon provided or a clean knife and dip into the open salt. Gently tap the spoon or knife over the food you desire to season. Remember to taste food before seasoning.

Spaghetti: Italians eat a few strands at a time by twirling the spaghetti hand. As you twirl the spaghetti around, hold it against the spoon. Place the spoon on the plate and carefully lift the fork to your mouth.

RESTAURANT DINING

CHECKING YOUR COAT
The gentleman you are with, including your father and brother, should check his coat if there is a coat room. As a lady, you will take your coat to the table. Check your umbrella and any large packages.

THE MAITRE D'HÔTEL
Wait until the headwaiter, the "maitre d'," seats you. Ladies follow first. If no one shows you to your table, the gentleman leads. The gentleman always leads when leaving the restaurant.

BEING SEATED
If there is no maitre d' to pull out the lady's chair, the gentleman she is with assists her. My brothers always did this for my twin sister and me.

A gentleman seats a lady in a chair with a good view. When two women are dining, the older woman gets the best view. This rule applies when one woman is much older than the other, say, a mother and her daughter or a teacher and a student.

YOUR PURSE

Never place your purse on the table. Place it on your lap or under your chair.

ORDERING

Before ordering, ask your dinner companion or family members what looks good to them. If you do not understand something, ask questions. Avoid ordering the most expensive item, unless you are certain that the cost does not matter to the person taking you out to eat. Avoid, also, ordering the cheapest item on the menu because your host may get the impression you think he is cheap.

Don't complain if you are on a diet. Order what you should eat without making it the topic of conversation.

If other guests order a course that you do not want to eat, you do not need to order it. If you do not desire to eat an appetizer, for example, and everyone else does, then don't be pressured into ordering one. While they are eating, this is a good time to try out your conversational skills. Remember to have some "conversational starters" thought out before the evening begins.

Unlike private homes, you may ask for anything you do not see on the table, such as catsup or other condiments.

COMPLAINTS

Any complaints about the food or service should be handled quietly and politely by the host (the person paying the bill).

CONVERSATION

Your conversation during your meal should be quiet. Even repeated loud laughter can be annoying to others.

GREETING OTHERS

If friends stop by your table, the gentlemen at your table stand, unless they are in a booth. If you pass by someone you know, either on the way in or out, you may stop and say a brief hello. Reserve long conversations for another time.

DOGGIE BAG

You may ask for a "doggie bag" if you cannot eat all of your food. Leftover portions are said to go in doggie bags, because people use to take leftover home to their dogs. Most of us, however, enjoy these leftovers for ourselves. Sorry Fiddo!

Never use doggie bags when eating a buffet meal. You do not take food from the buffet table and take it home. This also applies to weddings or other functions where food is set out on serving tables. Never take "one for the road."

THE BILL

When the bill arrives, the thoughtful young woman of confidence excuses herself to the ladies room so her host can figure out the bill, privately. Don't stand next to your host if he pays at the cash register. Go stand near the door or at least a few feet away. The waiter should receive about a 15% tip for his service. Figure the tip on the amount before taxes. If the service was exceptional, make your tip more than 15%. Some restaurants automatically include the tip in the bill, so check before tipping.

In our family, whoever peeks at the bill, gets to pay it -- so my children and I are careful not to pry into these business matters. On occasion, we tell them how much the meal costs so they can practice figuring out an appropriate tip for the waiter.

GOING DUTCH

Many times when you eat out, everyone pays for their own meal. Sometimes on a date, the young lady pays for her half of the check. This is called "going dutch" or "dutch treat." Know who is paying the bill before you enter a restaurant.

LEAVING

As you leave the restaurant, be sure to thank your waiter. If you enjoyed the meal, say so. If the service was exceptionally good, tell the maitre d' or hostess. When there is a comment card on the table, take a minute to fill it out. Restaurants desire your repeat business so need to know their strengths and weaknesses.

HOME DINING

Home entertaining can be anything you want it to be. You can treat your guests to a formal sit-down dinner or enjoy a casual meal, such as a barbecue. Whatever type of meal you decide to serve, always make your guests feel at home -- the key to good manners.

CASUAL ENTERTAINING

These are meals where guests become involved. Someone may offer to toss the salad and another guest might serve the beverages. Any host at the barbecue knows that he will have several "advisors" to help with the cooking. Guests don't mind helping themselves at casual dinners, but they should know what food and beverages are available and where anything else is they might need.

You can eat casual meals anywhere. You can have your guests sit around a fondue pot at the kitchen table and cook their own food. They can enjoy Chinese food, sitting on floor cushions in front of a roaring fire. Picnics in the backyard or park are fun, as well as finger foods in front of the television for an important football game.

For a formal sit-down dinner, the guests do not become involved with clean up. For casual dining, guests often help clear the table and put away the food. This, of course, depends on the hostess. Some women do not like other people in their kitchens.

A shy friend appreciates the opportunity to help. When she feels useful, she will usually relax enough to do a little talking -- at least in the kitchen.

Some of my most enjoyable meals have been casual and planned at the last minute. "We are cooking hamburgers on the grill and have plenty. Would you like to join us?" "We are going to have an ice cream sundae building contest. Why don't you bring your family over and join us later on this evening?"

BUFFETS

A buffet is a meal consisting of the food set out in serving dishes and placed on a table, counter top, or buffet where the guests serve themselves. These types of meals can be more formal, where the guests sit at a pre set table after serving themselves. Buffets can also be informal where the guests eat their food from lap trays, sitting here, there and everywhere. You may eat a buffet meal from a standing position. The food should be such that a knife is not necessary.

Buffet meals are great ice breakers. People always talk to one another while serving food. The guests can serve as much or as little food as they like. Thirdly, the guests can serve themselves seconds (when offered) so the hostess can keep the conversation going with the remaining guests.

I always have extra food for buffet meals, since guests seem to eat more when they serve themselves.

One important rule. Don't overload your plate at a buffet meal. The owner of a local French restaurant told my husband and me that, "Although Americans invented the buffet meal, they do not know how to serve themselves properly. They pile the food on their plates as though this was their last meal, and they usually waste a good portion. They should, instead, serve themselves salad and go eat it. Then they may return to the buffet for the rest of the meal without overloading their plates. After they have enjoyed this portion of the meal, they may return for seconds or dessert."

Have you ever been at the end of a buffet line somewhere, only to discover that most of the food was gone before you had a chance to serve yourself? I have. Please be considerate of others. Be courteous and serve yourself a moderate amount.

Although a female guest is usually first in a buffet line with the hosts last, all the females don't have to go through the line before the gentlemen.

Whoever happens to be standing nearest to the food, follows next in line. A gentleman is thoughtful if he sees to a lady's beverage after they have both served themselves.

TABLE SETTING FOR A BUFFET

Cover your buffet table, kitchen counter, or whatever you use to serve the buffet meal with a bright table cloth or runner. Be creative and use a Mexican blanket for a Mexican dinner, or floral fabric for a ladies' luncheon. You can make your centerpiece or your main dish your focal point.

Whether you have one or two serving lines, set the plates at the end of the table, then the main course, vegetables, salad, condiments (salt, pepper, butter), and rolls. The silverware and napkins are at the end of the buffet. You may roll the silverware in the napkin or place it alongside the napkin.

Serve dessert and coffee from the same buffet table after it has been cleared. You may also serve dessert from a different table, or bring it out to each guest.

THE SIT-DOWN DINNER

Sit-down dinners don't have to be stiff and uncomfortable if you use your imagination.

To get the conversation going, give your guests something to talk about as they approach the table. You can use an unusual centerpiece that they might comment on. An ice bucket filled with the salad is creative. You can use different colors and sizes of candles placed on a mirror or a favorite collection, such as various porcelain butterflies. A grouping of your favorite collection will start your guests talking about their own collections.

Sometimes I like to fold everyone's napkins differently. One evening, my guests became enthused napkin folders and requested lessons.

A good idea, for your menu, is to prepare one fantastic dish. This could be the main course, a special salad and dressing or an extravagant dessert. My Chocolate Mocha Cheesecake does the trick every time I prepare it. Your special dish will give your guests something to talk about as well as enable you to fix easier dishes for the rest of the meal.

A sit-down dinner will be more interesting if you invite people who get along but who are not all alike. If you invited all quiet friends, who would keep the conversation going? You and you alone! If everyone was the talkative type, who would do the listening? Think carefully when you plan your guest list.

When the conversation does die down at any given time, the hostess is responsible for starting it up again. Since I am not quick on my feet when under pressure, I will usually have rehearsed a few questions or comments on current events before my guests arrive. Conversation starters are oh so helpful.

Remember to include all of your guests in the conversation without allowing any one person to monopolize the conversation.

If the conversation is lively at the table, don't cut it off by serving dessert in the living room. Serve your dessert at the table.

Your guests will know that you think they are special if you concentrate on making them feel comfortable rather than focusing on your own pleasures. They will want to come back. When I know that my guests are enjoying themselves, I have a good time and do not even think about all the hard work spent to make the evening a success.

FORMAL DINNER PARTY
The formal dinner includes engraved invitations which are sent out and the guests expected to wear formal attire (long gowns and tuxedos). Four or five courses are served with two or three types of wine. The hostess does not serve her guests, but has a waiter dressed in a uniform do the serving.

Entertain in the way you feel most comfortable. Having friends over should be a pleasant experience. You are a confident host/hostess when you know that your guests are enjoying themselves. By concentrating on bringing out the best in your friends, you will shine.

REVIEW
Dining Etiquette

1. Where is the salad plate placed if served with the entree? ("Placing Your Silverware and Dishes") _____.

2. Do you need a salad fork if the salad is served with the entree? ("Placing Your Silverware")   Yes or No

3. You should always blot your lips with your _____ before you take a _____.

4. When at someone else's house, do you say grace if the hostess does not? Yes or No

5. Take the first piece of food you _____ ("Serving")

6. Who eats first? ("Who Eats First")_____

7. May you butter your entire roll all at once? ("Bread and Butter")
 Yes or No

8. How many pieces of meat do you cut at a time? _____

9. What is the Finished Position for your fork and knife?

_____

10. In a restaurant, if you drop something on the floor, what do you do?
_____. In someone else's home?

_____

11. Are frenchfries always finger foods? Yes or No

12. Where does a lady place her purse when dining out?

_____

13. In someone's home, if you don't see something on the table, may you ask for it? ("Ordering")   Yes or No

14. How much of a tip should a waiter receive? _____

15. What is one important rule when serving yourself at a buffet? ("Home Dining: Buffets") _____

Dear Parent,

Family mealtime should afford family members an opportunity to relax, enjoy a good meal, and share activities, feelings, and ideas. To watch someone totally "pig out" at the table can ruin a person's appetite. An enjoyable meal may also be disrupted when a family member is continually harassed for poor table manners. One of my students once told me, "Life would be easier if we didn't have to eat (and get yelled at)."

Don't strive for perfection today or even tomorrow. Focus on one or two table manners at a time so your son or daughter does not become overwhelmed with dining rules. As he/she masters one skill, such as chewing with his mouth closed or keeping her elbows off the table, add a new dining guideline to the list. Encourage efforts and gently remind him/her of forgotten manners. Humiliation, even in front of other family members, only leads to discouragement.

Bon appétit!

Deborah Wuerslin

LIFE LINE
Implementing Excellence

Inside Out

God has given each of you some special abilities; be sure to use them to help each other, passing on to others God's many kinds of blessings.
1 Peter 4:10 Living Bible

You are a unique person -- different from anyone else in this world. Your personality has its own characteristics and temperament. Your thoughts, your dreams, your likes and dislikes belong to you.

God combined your uniqueness with special abilities when he created you. He gave you some natural talents. He also opens doors where you can develop new skills. Some skills, such as tennis, may be for your enjoyment. Other skills, such as electronics, will help you on your job. God gave us all of these abilities, however, to share with others.

Jesus was never selfish. Although he stole some private time to draw from the Father, he shared all that he had. He looked to the welfare of others.

You cannot out give God. The more love and time you share, the more God will pour into your life. Fulfillment in life comes from giving and reaching out.

I am not fully dressed until I adorn myself with a smile.
Unknown

INSIDE OUT

As in your personal style on how your dress, you also have a personal style in how you speak and relate to others. By focusing on your positive personal style and your inward confidence, you will begin reflecting outwardly in your appearance and actions.

Just as you look in a mirror to discover your positive physical attributes, take a look at your inner self. Learn what your special skills and talents are. Outward looks change, but inner loveliness continues to blossom.

For the sake of clarification, a skill is a learned art in accomplishing something competently. A skill develops with practice. Cooking, sewing, playing sports, writing stories, making speeches, and playing a musical instrument are examples of skills.

A talent is a natural tendency, an ability with which you are born. Some call a talent a gift. Examples of talents are the ability to make people laugh or feel comfortable in their surroundings. The knack for encouraging and raising the spirits of a losing team. A gift for calming an angry mob or comforting a sad friend.

SKILLS

I have a skill in organization. I can organize a banquet practically with my eyes closed. This is a skill that developed with experience. I learned from my mistakes and improved on my arrangements. Rather than hide my skill in organization, I share my skill with churches, schools, clubs and neighborhoods. I even teach my students in my course, "Quest For Excellence," how to plan parties, set a table, entertain within a budget, and how to organize a guest room. They learn how to organize their closets and drawers, and acquire techniques in writing letters, organizing speeches, and becoming effective speakers.

212

Perhaps you developed a skill in acting. You might feel confident enough to help produce school or church plays. How about organizing a play or talent show for a local nursing home.

You might be a skillful horseback rider. What a blessing for a little blind child or underprivileged children to be able to ride a horse with you. They would be thrilled at their one opportunity to share a ride on your horse.

After several seasons of tennis, you might have developed a skill for the game. Share your learned techniques by practicing with an inexperienced player.

Don't wait to perfect your skill before you decide to share it. You will encourage others with whatever amount of abilities you share.

TALENTS

Are you gifted with a keen mind? Does school work come easily for you? You could help a classmate who is having trouble with his or her schoolwork.

You might have a creative mind. You could share this talent by designing posters for a friend's campaign for student council President. Perhaps you have a knack for stretching your wardrobe by combining different tops, skirts, and pants. Help your friend.

Although all of us should have a positive attitude, some people have a gift for seeing good in any situation. They spread their cheer wherever they go.

Some have the tendency to comfort and share kindness with others. Maybe you have a special gift for encouraging others or bringing peace into their lives with your quiet, gentle spirit.

You might be at ease with meeting people and making them feel comfortable in their new surroundings. How about the gift of friendship? You know how to meet the needs of those around you.

People appreciate a trustworthy individual. You could be very dependable, willing and determined to see a project through to the end.

213

Perhaps you can be relied upon to take care of a neighbor's pet while they are on vacation or weed a flower bed, no matter how hot the weather becomes.

Your patience with younger children might give you responsibilities in working as a teacher's aide.

DISCOVER YOUR SKILLS AND TALENTS

The list could go on and on. But what about you? Take the time to write down all of YOUR special skills and talents. You will begin to discover your personal style in how you relate to others. You will find that your life will be more exciting. You will blossom into a true young woman of confidence or mature into a gentleman of nobility.

No two people are exactly the same. Appreciate the different skills and talents in others.

> I love to hear a funny joke and have a good laugh. I appreciate my family and friends for tickling my funny bone. I am not a good joke teller. Rather than trying to be something I am not, I don't strive to tell funny jokes. I encourage the humor of these comedians by relaxing in my role as a good listener.

DEVELOP NEW SKILLS

> When spring track season ended, Timothy Chad's neighborhood swim club invited him to join their summer swim team. Although he had never competed in swimming before, he accepted the invitation. He decided to use this opportunity to build stamina and strengthen his muscles for fall cross country. Through hard work and determination, Timothy developed a new skill and became one of the fastest free-style swimmers on his team.

> Upon retirement, Larry and Kathy Woods purchased a canoe. They desired to enjoy the outdoors as well as keep in shape. After lessons and months of canoeing trips, they became skilled at maneuvering their canoe through rapids. The Woods did not allow age to become a roadblock. As long as they were in good health, they knew that you are never too old to learn new skills.

Don't be content with just your present skills. As opportunities present themselves, develop additional skills.

CONTINUALLY TRY TO DISCOVER NEW TALENTS

> I discovered my talent for working with children only after I agreed to teach Sunday School for a year. If I had allowed my inadequacies to rule me, I never would have consented to teach. Instead, I decided to accept the challenge. I soon discovered my talent for effectively communicating to children through my animated style of teaching and love and patience in working with young people. My organizational skills enabled me to effectively plan for my classes, keeping every hour running smoothly.

Practice the social skills taught in "Quest For Social Excellence." You will gain confidence in handling yourself with friends and adults. As you become more relaxed, you will be able to focus more on sharing your skills and talents with others.

215

REVIEW
Inside Out

1. From the chapter, define "skill" and give two examples.

_____

_____

_____

2. Define "talent" and give an example.

_____

_____

3. Name one of your skills.
   a)

4. Name two skills you would like to develop.
   a)
   b)

5. What talent do you possess? _____

6. How can you use this talent? _____

Inside Out

Dear Parent,

Begin to help your son or daughter discover his/her gifts and develop his/her talents by communicating love and acceptance. Encourage his/her efforts so frustration won't set in for not achieving an immediate goal.

If you reward only for a well-done, completed task, he/she will learn to measure worth by perfection. Encourage efforts and improvement. Realizing perfection is not a must, persistence will become the focus, and confidence will grow in trying to develop new skills.

Motivate your son or daughter to share gifts and talents with others rather than cultivating talents for personal gain. His/her contributions help others function more positively.

In his book, "Parents Who Encourage, Children Who Succeed," Dr. Highlander says, "Encouragement cultivates enriching values and goals in life. It builds healthy self-esteem, self-confidence, and good behavior."

Deborah Wuerslin

LIFE LINE
Implementing Excellence

Close Encounters

Be devoted to one another in brotherly love. Honor one another above yourselves.
Romans 12:10 NIV

Live in harmony with one another; be sympathetic, love as brothers, be compassionate and humble.
1 Peter 3:8 NIV

A friend loves at all times.
Proverbs 17:17a NIV

Encourage one another and build each other up.
1 Thessalonians 5:11 NIV

God gives us opportunities to share our confidence in him in our everyday lives. Our family, friends, and neighbors all need God's love.

The personal and social skills in "Quest For Excellence," help to equip you with confidence. Combine this confidence with an inward growth in the Lord, and you will be prepared to reach out to others. Your consideration of other will come more naturally.

Family members might let you down and friends might hurt you, but your joy and confidence in Him are to remain in Him.

One of the best places to practice thoughtfulness is in the home.
Deborah Wuerslin

Close Encounters

FAMILY COURTESY

Enjoying a pleasant atmosphere in your home doesn't just happen. You have an active part. Showing the same kindness and consideration to the members of your family as you do to your friends, is a sign of healthy self respect and common courtesy.

Good communication helps to develop meaningful relationships with your family members. If a best friend would move far away, you would set aside time to write letters to him or her. You would remain close to your friend by continuing to share your feelings, activities, dreams, and even your problems. Rather than writing letters to your family, ask your parents if you can set aside a regular time where you all can communicate with one another. You'll become a support group for one another by better understanding each another. You'll learn how to encourage and comfort each other.

> A particular family whom I know includes eight children, all involved in many activities. They all look forward to their Sunday afternoon "Round Table." This ten-member family plots their weekly calendar with social activities, chores, and school-assignment deadlines. They discuss family and personal problems, set goals, and deliver praises. They always take time to share compliments and words of appreciation with one another. Good communication makes this family a close-knit group.

You and your family can practice the communication skills outlined in "Conversations". Take turns at mealtime and play host or hostess. Remember, your responsibility as the host or hostess is keeping the conversation flowing.

Every family experiences stress. A good counterbalance for tension is playing together. Set aside a weekly "Family Night: and take turns planning activities--games, showing home movies, outdoor activities or outings. Does your family have a busy schedule? You might need to schedule a night together on the calendar. Dating your family is fun and will build a treasure of happy and special memories.

Other ways to help make your household a happy one are:
- Always address your parents with respect: "Yes, Mom," "Yes, Dad," "Yes, Mam," or "Yes, Sir" rather that "O.K." or "Yeah."
- Hold a door open for your parents.
- Allow your parents to enter a room first.
- Be courteous to your parents' friends. A few kind words are always thoughtful.
- Know and keep family rules and do not complain about them to your friends, unless they are demeaning of abusive.
- Do not share family secrets with your friends.
- Make sure an activity you want to participate in does not conflict with the family calendar. Check with your parents before committing yourself to an activity.
- Do not ask your parents if a friend can come to your house with your friend standing nearby. No need to cause embarrassment to your friend if the answer is "No."
- Be responsible in even small areas of responsibility -- chores, being on time.
- Be dependable and honest.
- Respect the privacy of others in your family. Knock on closed doors. Do not snoop though another family member's belongings or mail.
- Do favors. Helping family members with their chores gives you more time to spend together or enables them to participate in an activity in which they might not have had time.
- Treat your brothers and sisters as good friends. Compliment them rather than criticizing them.
- Return anything borrowed in good shape and good repair. Return and borrowed clothing cleaned and ironed.
- After you use the family car, put in some gas and clean out your trash.

- Do your share of picking up. Your room may not bother you, but may cause aggravation with your parents. When your room is clean and orderly, you can find things easier.
- Bathroom: No towels on the floor. Clothes picked up. Bathtub cleaned out. Personal items put away (makeup, hair brushes, toothpaste).
- Wipe your feet before coming inside.
- Walk through the house without running your hands along the walls.
- When you don't understand someone, avoid "Huh?" Ask, "I'm sorry, I didn't understand you. Would you please say that again?" "Excuse me?" "Pardon me.?"
- Thank you notes to family members are always appreciated. Send flowers or gifts on special occasions.
- An occasional love note will brighten someone's day.

Friends are forever because they can tell us the best and worse in us and still be our friends.
-Dr. Don Highlander

FRIENDS

As you practice building solid relationships in your family, you will learn how to be a good friend in other social friendly relationships. Good friends are important persons in your lives. They make the transition from living at home to being on your own much easier. Friends are your support group outside of your family.

Friends share activities together as well as secrets. Friends share fun times. Friends also encourage one another during rough times. Friends outside of your home can bring different ideas and interests into your relationship, enriching your life.

A special friendship grows when you work at it. Apply the conversation skills taught in this book. Show interest in your friends by asking them questions about themselves. If they are involved in a sport, ask:

What type of skills are required?

Why did they become involved in this sport?

Who do they enjoy this sport with?

How well are their skills improving?

When and Where will they be competing so you can go cheer them on?

- Remember not to ask a question that can be answered with a simple yes or no.
- When your friend is sick, offer to get his homework assignments. Make him a get-well card. Be a thoughtful friend.
- Did your friend ask you for your opinion? Answer directly and truthfully. Be an honest friend.
- Teach your friend a skill, craft, or sport you enjoy. Be a sharing friend.
- Did your friend lose an important competition? Send him a "Cheer up!" balloon. Tell him that you are proud of him for trying so hard and know he will do better next time. Be an encouraging friend.
- Don't keep talking about how wonderful you are at a particular activity. Don't be a boastful friend.
- Return anything you borrow as soon as possible. Make sure that the item is in as good or better condition than when you borrowed it. Don't wait for your friend to ask you for the item. Be a considerate friend.
- Don't expect your friend to get rid of a bad habit overnight. Perhaps she continually interrupts people when they are talking or arrives late for appointments. Be a patient friend.
- Apologize after a disagreement or for upsetting your friend. when your feelings get hurt, remember to be a forgiving friend.

- Learn to keep a secret. Don't share private information entrusted to you by a friend with someone else. Be a respectful friend.
- When your friend is hurting or sad, give her a hug and a kind word. Be a comforting friend.
- Allow your friend to cultivate other friendships. Don't be a jealous or possessive friend.
- Don't make fun of your friend for being afraid to try an activity you enjoy. Be an understanding friend.
- Don't keep your friend waiting unnecessarily. Be known for your punctuality. If you are going to be late, call and explain. Be a courteous friend.
- Keep a promise. If you said you would do something, do it. Be a faithful friend.
- Stick to your values. If a friend wants you to do something that you feel isn't right, don't join your friend. Be a friend with steadfast convictions.
- Don't gossip with or about your friend. Be a trustworthy friend.
- Don't walk away from your friend to be with another (male or female). Include your friend or tell the other friend that you will see him or her later. Be a committed friend and you will earn the respect of others.
- Look for the positive qualities in your friend and give him/her compliments. Be a motivating friend.

The key to an enduring friendship is to treat your friend the same way in which you would like to be treated, or better. If they abuse your generosity, set limits. However, guard your attitude and keep your mind open.

Those who bring sunshine to the lives of others cannot keep it from themselves.
--James Barrie

AMONG NEIGHBORS

Although you may not be best friends with all of your neighbors, be friendly towards them all. Help to make your neighborhood a pleasant place in which to live.

> A new neighbor recently told me that she finally made the decision to buy the house across the street because of one of my children. When she returned to look at the house for the second time, she notice a group of girls and boys playing basketball across the street, next door to my house. She got out of her car, and a very friendly teenager waved to her and shouted, "Hello!" This impressed my neighbor. She decided that this must be a friendly neighborhood to live in so she bought the house.

You may never know how your friendliness towards your neighbors makes a difference in their lives. One thing is for sure, your pleasant smile and kind words will make your neighbors enjoy their surroundings a little bit more.

MORE FRIENDLY TIPS
- Whenever you hear of a neighbor in need, find out whether you or someone in your family can help.
- Offer a ride to a neighbor whose car won't run.
- Show thoughtfulness by picking up an elderly neighbor's newspaper from the curb and placing it on his front porch.
- Offer to pick up your neighbors' mail and newspapers during their vacation.
- Respect your neighbor's property by not walking through his yard without permission.
- Keep your animals in your own yard. Train them to be friendly but not to jump on others. Walk your dog on a leash and don't

allow it to fulfill its call of nature in someone else's yard. Make sure that your cherished pet doesn't disturb the neighbors. If a neighbor complains, assure them that you care and appreciate their willingness to complain.

- Playing music outdoors is entertaining, but make sure that it does not disturb your neighbors.
- If you borrow an item from a neighbor, ask when you can return it.

I was to teach dining etiquette to a group of women, when I realized that I didn't have my card table. I had loaned my table to a neighbor two months earlier. To my dismay, I discovered that this neighbor was out of town. I needed a table on which to display my place setting. Consequently, I had to borrow a card table from someone else.

Another time I loaned an appliance to a neighbor. This particular item was returned broken. I knew that this family could not afford to replace the appliance. I just learned to live without it.

- Don't borrow anything that you can't afford to replace. You wouldn't want to do anything to cause friction or hard feelings with one of your neighbors.
- How thoughtful to return a casserole dish with homemade cookies inside. Show your appreciation in some way when you borrow something. A thank you note sometimes is appropriate in showing gratitude.
- Speak well of your neighbors. If you have nothing nice to say, say nothing. Any negative words you say will eventually come back to you.
- Help to keep your yard looking presentable and attractive. Nothing irritates neighbors more than to have to look at a yard full of tall grass and weeds. A resident in Germany will receive a ticket for not keeping the street in front of his house swept. Keep your driveway and curb swept clean even if you will not have to pay a fine for not doing so. Celebrate Earth Day with a positive mental attitude to clean up and keep up your home and yard appearance.
- On a walk and see a piece of trash? Pick it up and dispose of it properly. Take pride in your neighborhood.

•Learn to say hello to your neighbors by name. Adults, today, are pleasantly surprised when a young person greets them. Devise creative ways to remember names and for introducing yourself to others.

> A few years ago, I drove my son to a birthday party. When I dropped him off, I got out of the car to congratulate the birthday boy and greet the hosting parent. Not one of the seven or eight boys playing on the front lawn said a word to me, not even the birthday boy.

Take the time to be a friendly neighbor. "Research reveals that the higher level of social interest and friendliness, the higher the level of emotional health and personal fulfillment. There is also a direct correlation between success and friendly behaviors." (Research paper by D.H. Highlander, Ph.D., Georgia State University)

Politeness includes ease and freedom; it simply consists in treating others just as you love to be treated yourself. Give to others what you would like to receive if you were in the receiving position.

BEING A GOOD SPORT

Sports were originally organized as a training ground for war. During peaceful times sports developed into an opportunity for friendly competition.

Winning is attitude and behavior, not just being #1. Unfortunately, some people forget about friendly competition and act as though winning is a matter of life and death. They forget that how you play is equally important as to whether you win or lose.

Play your best, clothed in a positive, enthusiastic attitude. When you are winning, don't rub it in to your opponent or opposing team. If you are losing, continue to play your best. You may not feel like cheering. But you don't need to act grumpy or display a temper. Lose with dignity and learn from your mistakes.

When sitting on the bench, be a good sport. Sit with pride. Pay attention and cheer your team onward. As one sportsman said, "It's never over until it's over."

Resolve any conflicts with your coach or teammates as soon as possible.

A team sport involves interaction between players on the same team. There is no time for grandstanding. You and your teammates are to work together. You'll have a stronger team if one person isn't trying to score all the points. Your opponents are often fooled most by teamwork and active support.

Treat opposing team members as guests rather than enemies. Learn to value their strengths and skills as well as those of your own team.

Be an encourager. Cheer up a discouraged teammate. "Don't worry about that (missed) shot. You'll get the next one." Stay focused.

Compliments inspire teammates to work harder. "Wow! Your overhead shots (in tennis) have really improved." "You can tell you've been practicing your jumps (in ice skating). Your landings are a lot smoother."

Compliment a teammate or opponent on a skillful play during the game. "Great shot." "You guys sure work well together." "What teamwork!"

In "Parents Who Encourage, Children Who Succeed," D.H. Highlander, Ph.D., states, "Encouragement cultivates enriching values and goal in life. It builds healthy self-esteem, self-confidence, and good behavior." He says encouragement is:

- The feeling that comes when someone says, "I like the way you do that. Mind if I watch?"
- The confidence that I am loved for who I am and not just for what I can do,
- The knowledge that, no matter what happens, I'm accepted and needed as an indispensable part of my family,

- The assurance from someone I love that it's all right if I make a mistake because that's the way I learn,
- The conviction that I as a person am more important that the problems I get involved in,
- The acceptance of an honest appraisal that leaves me challenged to grow rather than condemned to fail.

Encourage your teammates, realizing you are seeking a common goal--satisfaction of a game well played. Criticism only dampens team spirit.

Show respect to your coach and try to learn from each practice session. Be on time for practices and follow his or her rules. If you disagree with a decision, talk to your coach privately and courteously. It is not wise to put your coach on the defensive.

A coach needs reassurance that he is doing a good job. Thank him for his time and efforts. Your gratitude will motivate your coach to continue even though your team may not be winning.

Do not question a referee's judgment. He usually has a lot more experience than you do. Realize that every referee seeks to call games to the best of his ability. His job is to assure that a safe and fair game is played.

Never yell at a referee. You might find yourself thrown out of a game. Your rudeness and temper will hurt your entire team. Your coach can protest a game if he feels the referee has not applied the rules of the game properly.

Learn the rules of the game or sport in which you participate and abide by them.

One last word. Be a responsible teammate. Make sure you have any equipment, clothing, or accessories you need. We all borrow from a teammate once in awhile, but don't make borrowing a habit.

When I was in a dance company, fellow dancers were constantly borrowing safety pins and bobby pins from me before performances. Sometimes they didn't even bother to ask first. One time I needed a safety pin and there was not one to be found.

Be an example to your team by being a good sport. A favorite saying of mine is, "Because there is a drop of rain, don't let it cloud the sun." Your performance in sports may not meet your expectations. Don't allow your disappointing achievements, however, to affect your behavior on the team. Continue to spread sunshine with a positive attitude and encouraging words. Be a good sport.

REVIEW
Close Encounters

1. How can you prevent an activity of yours from conflicting with the family calendar? ("Family")

_____

2. When you don't understand someone, what is a good response? ("Family")_____

3. When a friend asks you for your opinion, what should you do? ("Friends")

_____

4. What do you do if a friend asks you to participate in activity you don't feel is right? ("Friends")

_____

5. How can you respect your neighbor's property? ("Among Neighbors")

_____

6. How can you be considerate about outdoor music? ("Among Neighbors")

_____

7. Learn to say _____ to your neighbors by name. _____ enjoy young people greeting them. ("Among Neighbors")

8. When you are losing a game, continue to _____ _____, lose with _____, and _____ from your mistakes. ("Being A Good Sport")

9. You can show respect to your coach by: a) _____, b) _____, c) _____

10. Even if a referee's calls are consistently in error, don't ever _____ at an official. ("Being A Good Sport")

231

Dear Parent,

Harmony within the family takes place when each member shows consideration towards one another. This family courtesy begins with effective and regular communication. "Close Encounters" offers suggestions for sharing feelings, ideas, dreams, and problems.

Read the guidelines with your son or daughter on ways to show thoughtfulness around the home. Add to this list with input from every family member. Devise a reward system for implementing these courtesies. My husband and I added family courtesies to our young children's "Chores and Responsibilities" charts. So many stars meant special activities with Mom and Dad, sometimes corporately and other times on a one on one activity. As our children grew older, we treated them to special outings.

Congenial relationships begin in the family and extend into the neighborhood. Although he/she may not always be treated kindly and fairly, your son or daughter can learn to focus on his/her friendliness towards neighbors, classmates, and team members.

Reassure your son or daughter of your love for him/her despite occasional mistakes. Help him/her turn blunders and problems into learning and growing experiences.

Deborah Wuerslin

LIFE LINE
Implementing Excellence

Out And About

We are Christ's ambassadors
2 Corinthians 5:20a Living Bible

"Out and About" takes the guess work out of how to behave out in public. When you learn how to respond in different social situations, you will relax and be able to be yourself -- a child of God who can enjoy himself and remain courteous and outgoing.

As you represent the Lord, your family, community and country when out in public places, you will make mistakes. *And we know that in all things God works for the good of those who love him, who have been called according to his purpose.* Romans 8:28 NIV. God is true to his Word. He turns tragedies into victories. He can teach you lessons of eternal worth from mistakes you've made. God cares about his children. His purposes will be fulfilled in spite of our pain.

People you meet may not remember your name or the clothes you wore, but I hope they will say, "That young man (or young lady) radiates a special kind of joy. Did you notice how confident he seems?"

Make sure that your heart shines above all else. When you continually groom your heart by buffing it with a good coat of God's love and his Word, it will shine so much that others will see it above all else. Others will know you for your loving heart, your ability to reach out and your reputation for learning the "heart" of personal interest in others' lives and well being.

You are an ambassador wherever you go. You have opportunities to represent the qualities, traits, and habits of your family, neighborhood, school, state, and country.
-Deborah Wuerslin

OUT AND ABOUT

BEACH AND POOL

The beach and pool create an atmosphere for relaxing, socializing, and fun and laughter.

One thoughtless person can ruin someone else's good time, so be considerate and aware of other sunbathers and swimmers.

RULES
Before swimming or using the beach, read the rules.

Do your running on a part of the beach where you will not kick sand on anyone. Wrestle, play ball, or throw a frisbee away from others. You or your ball could knock into someone.

> When I was six months pregnant with my first child, I visited my parents in California. Naturally, we drove to the beach to enjoy a day of sun, surf, and sand. During our picnic lunch, a careless beachcomber threw a frisbee into my stomach. Yes, it hurt, but not as much as I thought my father was going to hurt those thoughtless boys. Dad kept his cool, but the boys did follow his advice to play elsewhere away from crowds of people.

Playing under the diving board might make an unpleasant "impression." Someone could accidentally jump on you.

Before you dive or jump into the pool, check to make sure no one is near where you plan to make your big splash.

Speaking of splash. Please don't splash others whether they are in or out of the water. Be kind to someone who doesn't know how to swim. Perhaps you can give a few pointers.

A lady always remembers to shave her legs and under her arms before she even thinks about wearing a swimsuit.

Wear your sunblock! Skin cancer is serious. Over tanning ages your skin. Ladies, remember your hair conditioner.

"The only thing you should leave on the beach are your footprints." Don't leave your litter on the beach or around the pool.

CHURCH

ARRIVING

Church is a special place for religious worship. Enter a church or synagogue in a reverent manner. Arrive before the service begins. If you arrive late, walk in quietly and sit near the back.

CHURCH ETIQUETTE

The entrance hall or "vestibule" lends itself for socializing before and after services. The sanctuary is set aside for group worship and private meditation rather than friendly conversations.

When in someone else's church, try to conform to the order of service by standing and sitting when others do. If you decide to remain seated, do not fidget. Look attentive. Slouching in your seat gives the impression you are bored. Good posture reflects a positive attitude.

Although you don't have to wear a dress or coat and tie to church, make sure your clothes are clean and pressed. Play clothes, such as shorts and halter tops are inappropriate. Dress modestly out of respect for God. Leave your shoes on at all times. A gentleman removes his hat.

Ladies and gentlemen carry a kleenex or handkerchief in their purse or pocket. You distract others by leaving the service for a kleenex. Tuck a few cough drops in your purse or pocket if you have a cough.

LEAVING

When leaving church, don't wait for people to greet you. Even if you are a visitor, introduce yourself to a few people. What an excellent opportunity to practice your social skills. Smile and use eye contact. Your friendliness might encourage a visitor to return next week.

> A woman in our church told her Sunday School class she returned to our church because of a caring teenager. She knew our church must be friendly because a young woman looked her in the eyes and kindly said, "I'm so glad you came to visit us today."

Speak to the minister on your way out if he is greeting at one of the exists of the church.

~~~~~~

HOSPITAL VISITOR

A hospital administers medical treatment to sick and injured people *24 hours a day*.

QUIET PLEASE

Be quiet in hospital halls because some patients may be sleeping. Many sick people are sensitive to sounds and are easily disturbed by visitors. Some patients are dying. Family and friends of the dying often sit in the halls and laughter can upset them.

CALL AHEAD

Call for visiting hours and to check the age limit. Respect the hospital rules and visit only during visiting hours.

Call the patient to ask if he or she can receive visitors. Some patients prefer to be left alone. If the patient desires to see you, ask for the best time (according to hospital visiting hours). Avoid mealtimes so the patient will feel free to eat.

Be sure flowers are O.K. to bring. They are often not allowed in the Intensive Care and Emergency Care Units. Also ask if the hospital has extra vases if you do not plan to bring your flowers in one.

Check with the nurse before bringing food. Many patients require special or restricted diets but will often tell you to bring food not allowed by their doctors.

If the nurse gives the all clear sign, offer to bring drinks and juice to the patient.

Offer to bring tapes, music, pillows, or pictures from home.

VISITING

Knock before entering.

Most hospitals limit two visitors at a time per patient. You must get permission to visit in a group.

> If the patient's roommate is trying to sleep, make your visit very brief. Once when I was in the hospital, my roommate had a visitor who was loud and stayed for the duration of visiting hours. This was my last chance for a good nap before I was to take my new baby home to meet his sister (3) and brother (22 months). Neither my roommate nor the visitor was sensitive to my needs. I became so frustrated that I walked out into the hall and cried.

Limit your visit to around ten minutes. Perhaps you are an out-of-town family member. Stay for short periods, then go to the waiting area, gift shop, or snack shop. Patients will often ask you to stay when they really need to rest. Rest helps the healing process, so keep your visits short.

Patients often appreciate calls more than visits. Make your calls short. If you can tell that someone has entered the patient's room (MD., nurse), offer to call later. Try to cheer up the patient but do not give out any advice. The doctors and nurses know how to best care for the patient.

Do not sit on or jar the patient's bed. Sick people are sensitive to motion, especially surgery patients.

Use the visitor's restroom in the hall rather than the patient's.

Do not play with equipment such as the beds, lights and IV equipment.

Do not eat or drink in front of a patient. And do not use a patient's ice or cup. If the doctor comes in, excuse yourself immediately. If the nurse comes in, ask if you need to leave. If you do leave, tell the patient where you will be and when you will be back. Again, knock when you return.

Offer to go the gift shop for the patient.

Don't talk "war stories." "When I was sick......When my mother was in the hospital..."

Please do not visit if you are sick, even with a slight cold.

Watch for restricted areas and service elevators and stay away. Hospitals use those elevators for emergencies and for surgical patients who are often going directly to surgery.

Do not ride elevators for fun.

GIFT IDEAS
Some gifts usually overlooked but really appreciated are: magazines, books, fruit, powder, hard candies, and personal items such as hand cream and chapstick. Unique gifts include pictures, cross stitch and other crafts, cassette tapes, a music box, major tricks for kids, puzzles, gift certificates, memo pad, stationery and stamps, address book, and recipe box including a few of your favorite recipes. Remember to have the nurse approve anything you bring to the patient.

The gift of time is very special. Offer to help the patient with school work. Offer to brush your friend's hair or apply a little makeup. She might appreciate a manicure. Play a game with him or her. For an adult, offer to babysit or run errands. For an older person, read a book.

Being sick is no picnic. Try to help a friend or family member who is in the hospital in any way you can. Be a comforter. Be a friend. Share your love.

~~~~~~~~~~~~~~~~~~~~~~~~~~~~~~~~~~~~~~

HOSPITAL PATIENT

We all would rather be a visitor in a hospital than a patient confined to a bed. Being sick can sometimes be a little frightening. When you find yourself as a patient, make the best of the situation.

Follow the doctors' and nurses' orders. They want to see your health improve quickly. Ask politely if you have any questions.

Make your ailments known to the staff, but do not continually complain. Even sick people can spread a little sunshine.

Do not press the call button for every little question. Try to save some of your comments and questions for when the nurse or doctor visits your room. Of course, ask any important questions or make any special requests right away.

It's not what you say but how you say it. Nothing is wrong with sharing a complaint if expressed in the right spirit.

> After the birth of my third child, I was trying to get a good night's sleep. This was the same day that I had tried in vain to take a nap. Around 11:30 p.m. the hospital staff just outside my door was apparently sharing funny stories. Their laughter was preventing my roommate and me from sleeping. I opened our door and stuck my head out and asked, "Excuse me. We are trying to sleep. We know you are

having a good time, but would you please laugh a little more softly?" I
asked politely and the nurses were very apologetic. I might not have
had the same response if I had flung open the door and yelled at them to
shut up.

Make sure you understand what your doctor allows you to eat or
drink. If a visitor brings you food or a beverage, check with the nurse before
accepting it.

Wear a bathrobe and slippers when your doctor permits you to walk
through the halls. Try to keep your hair and teeth brushed. If allowed, a
shower will make you feel and smell better.

Hospital staff appreciates hearing, "Please," and "Thank you."

BE A GOOD ROOMMATE
Exchange names with your roommate and briefly introduce him/her
to your visitors.

Be considerate of your roommate. If you cannot sleep, do not disturb
your roommate. Make as little noise as possible.

Be sensitive. Your roommate may not feel up to carrying on a
conversation. If you do not feel like talking, politely say so. Tell your
companion you normally enjoy talking but you are just not feeling up to it at
the moment.

THANK YOU
A thoughtful patient writes a thank you note to the hospital staff if
they have been exceptionally kind and sensitive to your needs. Your words of
gratitude will encourage the staff to continue to be caring and responsive to
other patients.

HOTELS AND MOTELS

What a treat to spend a night in a hotel or motel. Relaxing away from home can be fun. You can enjoy the pleasure of eating in a restaurant. And this is one time you don't have to make your own bed.

Please help the maid by keeping your belongings picked up. She is hired to clean your room and make your bed but not pick up after you.

Keep your voices, the radio, and the television low so as not to disturb your neighbors. Some guests sleep during the day so talk and walk quietly in the halls. Room service will deliver food to your room, but you will pay extra for this convenience. You will also want to tip the waiter for room service. Tip 15%, never less than 50 cents, unless the bill includes the tip.

Hotels offer services such as picking up clothes from your room to be laundered or pressed. They also deliver ice. Tip around 50 cents. If you get your own ice or take your own clothes to the valet, you do not need to tip.

A general rule of thumb for tipping a bell boy to carry suitcases to your room is to tip him 50 cents a suitcase and 25 cents for small bags, depending on the area of the country. Give the bell boy at least one dollar. Of course, a "Thank you" and a smile should accompany your tip.

Hotel ash trays and towels are not souvenirs. Taking these "mementos" is considered stealing. The postcards and stationary provided make nice remembrances of your vacation. You may also take the little hotel bar of soap, shower cap, or laundry bag provided.

LIBRARY

QUIET
Patrons desire a peaceful, quiet library. Making loud noises, laughing, or even carrying on a soft conversation disturbs people around you.

Be considerate. Allow the other library patrons to enjoy a good book or focus on a special project without interruption.

HELP!

Do you need assistance? Do not disturb anyone around you. Someone on the library staff will be happy to help you find what you are looking for.

CARING FOR BOOKS

Leave food, drinks, and gum outside the library. Clean hands will help keep books clean.

A book will last longer if the pages are not dog eared. Placing an opened book face down will break the binding. Use a bookmark to keep your place. Remember that a library book belongs to the public. Underlining and writing notations in the columns does not show respect for public property.

Return a book to its proper place if you decide not to check it out.

Return your books on time so that someone else may check them out.

Take advantage of your school and neighborhood libraries. Reading improves your mind and brings you hours of entertainment.

~~~~~~~~~~~~~~~~~~~~~~~~~~~~~~~~~~~~~~~

MOVIES

Below are some rules of etiquette that will make attending movies more enjoyable for you and those around you.

LINES

A friend or a date may drop you off at the theatre entrance to save a place in line. Do not save places for all of your friends who have not yet arrived. When friends arrive, either move to the back of the line with them or agree to meet them inside.

Purchase any refreshments and use the restroom before the movie begins so you do not disturb others during the movie. Lines are often long so allow for extra time.

QUIET PLEASE

Do not tap your foot on the chair in front of you.

Eat and drink quietly. Wait for a noisy scene before rattling candy wrappers.

Laughter is encouraged at appropriate times, but please do not make loud comments or chit chat with your neighbor.

Viewing home videos provides a relaxed atmosphere. Family and friends enjoy carrying on conversations, making comments, and chomping on favorite snacks. Unfortunately, this relaxed behavior has carried over into movie theatres. Please view a theatre movie in silence. Of course, laughing along with the audience adds to the enjoyment of the movie.

BE CONSIDERATE

Tuck your legs under your seat to allow someone to pass. A gentleman should stand only before or after the movie begins.

Reserve cuddling with your date for home movies. Be considerate of those behind you and do not block their view.

When the movie has ended, pick up your trash. Throw it away in the provided receptacles.

A smart moviegoer reviews a movie before attending. He saves himself and others the disappointment of walking out on an inappropriate film.

MUSEUMS

A building or a room that displays collections of objects for observation is a museum. These collections most often illustrate works of art, history, or scientific specimens.

QUIET PLEASE
Museums are quiet places where people like to study or ponder. Walk quietly through a museum. Never run, play or roughhouse with friends. Even giggling disturbs people.

Talk softly.

Read any literature to yourself so as not to disturb others.

SAVE THOSE FEET
Wear comfortable shoes. You can walk miles in a museum.

PRESERVE YOUR MUSEUM
Most museums require permission before taking pictures. They usually forbid flash bulbs and tripods

Some museums do not allow any use of writing or marking utensils during your museum tour.

Unless the museum has "hands-on" exhibits, never touch an object. Museum pieces last longer when not handled.

You must eat and drink only in designated areas.

BE ENLIGHTENED
You enhance your visit by prearranging for a guide to escort your group on a tour or taking the time to read any inscriptions next to the museum pieces. You leave the museum with a greater awareness and understanding of the world around you.

Take as long as you like to study a work of art. Stand back, however, so other patrons can view without obstruction.

SHOPPING

Shopping can be a pleasant experience filled with a sense of accomplishment. With poor planning, shopping wastes time and can turn into a disaster. Be prepared before you dash off to your favorite mall.

PLAN

Make a specific list of what you need to buy. Consider your finances. Do not make your list larger than your pocket book can handle. Decide which stores best suit your shopping needs. Stick to your list and do not get sidetracked.

Allow enough time for comparative shopping. You might find a lower price for the same item in another store. A pad and pencil will help keep track of the different stores, items, and prices.

DRESS FOR THE OCCASION

Soiled or play clothes, such as shorts and midriff-revealing tops, are not suitable for shopping. Research shows that salespeople will give you better service when you dress nicely and have a neat appearance.

Wear easily removable clothing for quick changes in the dressing rooms.

TALK SOFTLY

Talk softly in a store. Never call attention to yourself.

DON'T TOUCH

Shop with your eyes and not your hands. Handle merchandise only when you are seriously considering buying it.

NEATNESS COUNTS

If you unfold a garment, refold it and return it to its proper place. Did you knock a dress off its hanger? Hang it back up.

Take something out of a package only if you must. Put it neatly back in the package if you do not plan to buy it. Please do not litter the store with these wrappers and straight pins. Asking a salesperson for assistance would be wise.

PATIENCE IS A VIRTUE

Do not look at something someone else is examining. Wait until that person puts it down.

Do not interrupt the salesperson who is assisting someone else. Wait patiently. After the salesperson helps you, say "Thank you."

DRESSING ROOM ETIQUETTE

Hopefully, only a two year old who doesn't know any better, would look under someone else's dressing room door.

Clean up your mess in the dressing room. Return clothes you do not intend to buy to their original places or on the rack provided near the dressing room entrance. Walking into a cluttered dressing room frustrates a shopper.

BUY WISELY

The outfit you choose should be flattering in fit and color. Make sure that this outfit is dressy or casual enough for the planned occasion or activity.

Check the outfit for stains, tears, or missing buttons. Does the zipper work?

CHECKING OUT

Use eye contact and a smile when you greet the cashier. You could be the very person to brighten her long day.

Count your change. Be understanding if the cashier makes a mistake. Be honest and return any extra money.

People do notice good manners. They might not compliment you personally, but they will appreciate your gracious and thoughtful attitude.

~~~~~~

SPORTING EVENTS

Nothing is more exciting than to cheer on your favorite team to victory. Your enthusiasm for the sport, however, can offend some fans if you do not obey the sports rules of etiquette.

PUNCTUALITY
Arrive early to find your seat. Always allow extra time for the possibility of misplaced car keys, heavy traffic, or bad weather.

DO YOUR HOMEWORK
Know something about the sport before you attend the event. Ask any questions before the game begins. You might annoy your companion or other spectators by continually asking questions during the game.

SHOW RESPECT
Stand in a respectful manner for the national anthem, with no talking or fidgeting.

REFRESHMENTS
Eating during a sporting event is a good idea. Do remember to throw away your trash in the proper container.

If you are going out to eat after the game, you will not need to eat during the game. You may want to eat something, however, before you leave home. The game might run overtime.

WHAT TO WEAR

Find out where you are going after the game so you can dress appropriately. You will want to wear casual clothes to a sporting event. A sharp-looking pair of slacks or casual skirt would be in order. You will not want to wear jeans, though, if you are going somewhere other than a fast-food restaurant afterwards.

BE CONSIDERATE

If you must leave your seat, try to leave during a break in the game. You would not want to stand up and block the view of an exciting touchdown or homer. Your neighbors might decide to help you leave, a little faster than you expected!

Keep your belongings in your assigned seat area. This includes your feet. They never rest on the chair in front of you.

Try not to jump up and down with enthusiasm. You will block the view of the sport fans behind you.

Look interested even if the event bores you. Carrying on a conversation annoys your neighbors. Those around you do not want to listen to your pocket radio, either. If you must listen to another game, use headphones.

Be a good side-line sport. Never boo or yell at the referee. Cheer in an enthusiastic and positive manner for your favorite team.

~~~~~~

THEATRE

Attending a ballet, concert, or play is a special event. By learning how to behave at one of these special functions, you enable those around you to enjoy the performance as well.

DRESS FOR THE OCCASION

Play clothes are not appropriate for the theatre. A gentleman should wear a coat and tie and a "Sunday" dress for a lady. Wear dress shoes rather than sneakers. And always wear socks or pantyhose (no bare feet). Ladies, a bracelet, which makes noise by jingling, distracts other theatre patrons.

ARRIVING

I like to arrive at the theatre early. These extra minutes give me time to use the ladies room, get situated in my seat, and enjoy the company of my companion before the performance starts. Remember to allow for extra time for traffic and bad weather. If you arrive late, an usher might ask you to sit in the back row until intermission.

If you check your coat, be prepared to pay the fee plus a small tip of about 25 cents or as high as 75 cents or a dollar. When no charge is posted, tip about 50 cents for each coat. You do not need to tip for packages or umbrellas unless you require a lot of extra space.

THEATRE ETIQUETTE

A lady follows the usher to her seat with the gentleman following. When no usher seats you, the gentleman leads.

If you believe that someone is sitting in your seat, ask an usher to help you. Do not try to handle the situation yourself.

Face the stage when you pass in front of other seated guests. In Europe, theatregoers pass through a row by facing those already seated.

When someone passes in front of your seat, tuck your legs under your chair. If the performance has not started, a gentleman may stand slightly, pulling his seat in the upright position.

You may place your coat and purse on an empty seat only after the performance begins. During intermission, place your belongings on your own seat while you stretch your legs in the lobby.

Ladies and gentlemen always keep their shoes on in public places.

Talking during a performance is rude and prevents those nearby from hearing the performance properly.

Eating food during a performance bothers others. Some theatres prohibit eating in their auditorium.

Wait until intermission to enjoy some refreshments.

Be aware of the alloted time for the intermission so that you return to your seat before the performance begins.

Ladies, do not make a date spend the entire intermission by himself while you primp in the ladies room. He would rather your hair be a little messy and enjoy your company.

Applause is reserved for the end of each act in a play.

Each time the conductor enters the stage at a ballet or concert, the audience applauds. They become quiet when he turns his back to the audience. The audience holds their applause until he faces them again.

Sometimes the audience shows their enthusiasm by applauding a solo dance or pas de deux (a dance for two persons). Never applaud, however, after a musician plays a solo unless the conductor faces the audience.

Disrespectful theatregoers laugh at anyone's mistakes.

Have a kleenex or handkerchief on hand.

THE END
Gracious patrons wait until the entire performance is over before leaving. Making a mad dash to the parking lot is not well mannered. If you must leave early, leave quietly. Put your coat on in the lobby instead of at your seat.

Sometimes, we all attend a performance we do not enjoy. Enjoy the company of your friends, date, or family rather than dwelling on the negatives. If you decide to leave, wait until intermission.

At the end of the performance, remember to thank the person who accompanied you to the theatre. A grateful guest is invited again.

~~~~~~

TRANSPORTATION

AIR

An airplane is one of the fastest means of transportation. In the early days of travel, flights took over thirty hours to fly from one coast of the United States to the other, with many stops for refueling. Today you can fly from New York City to Los Angeles nonstop in about five hours.

Early passengers often had to sit on piles of mail bags. The flight conditions were less than desirable. Today, you can fly in comfort.

The following information will make your flight more enjoyable for you as well as your fellow passengers.

ARRIVAL

Check into the airport at least 30 minutes before scheduled flight time. Lines at airports are notoriously long.

Have your ticket ready when you get up to the counter.

LUGGAGE

Airline regulations allow you to check two pieces of luggage to go in the cargo area of the plane. Only two pieces of luggage can accompany you on the plane. These must fit either under your seat or in the overhead compartment.

If you checked your luggage at the outside curb, remember to tip the Skycap. A Skycap is the only airline employee whom you tip. If a flight attendant or other employee goes out of his or her way to help you, write a letter to the Director of Public Relations. On the ticket counters you will find a special form you can fill out.

WHAT TO WEAR

Wear comfortable clothes that do not wrinkle or snag easily. Play clothes are suitable for sports and play and not for traveling. For ladies, a dress, skirt, or dress slacks are appropriate to wear. Carry along a sweater or jacket in case you get chilled. For gentlemen, casual slacks with a polo or sport shirt is appropriate.

UP, UP, AND AWAY!

You may stop by the cockpit as you board. Pilots enjoy showing passengers their "office." Make your visit brief because the pilots have a great deal of work to complete before takeoff.

Find your assigned seat. Store your luggage and be seated. Fasten your seat belt.

Wait until the flight attendant walks by to ask for a pillow, blanket, or magazine. She might be busy helping people find their seats.

During takeoff, sit quietly during the flight attendant's safety instructions. Pay attention. This valuable information for emergencies may save your life.

You do not have to talk to the person seated next to you, but you can at least say a friendly, "Hello" as you sit down.

Travel with a book, magazine, or stationery. You will quickly pass the time by reading or by writing a letter to a friend. You can also use reading as an excuse if you do not desire to talk to the person next to you.

Remain seated for the duration of the flight unless you need to use the restroom. For longer flights, a brief walk in the aisle will relieve stiffness and restlessness.

TIME TO EAT

Remember your table manners.

Passengers usually talk to the person next to them during the meal portion of the flight. It is not necessary to share any personal information.

Do not ask for a second helping of food.

Say thank you when the flight attendant removes your food tray.

CALL BUTTON

The flight attendant will help you if you spill something and cannot manage the cleanup yourself. Press the flight attendant button and she will come to your seat.

Only use the flight attendant button when absolutely necessary. Flight attendants keep busy caring for all passengers.

LAVATORY

Make sure that you lock the door once inside the lavatory. You would not want the door to fly open while you are inside!

Other passengers may be waiting in line, so try not to spend too much time in the lavatory.

Wash your hands!

LIGHTS

Your own reading light is provided for your convenience. During an in-flight movie, turn your light out.

Passengers often sleep on the "all nighter." Be considerate and turn your light out. If you must read, move to a seat where there are no sleeping passengers nearby.

OTHER CONSIDERATIONS

Don't push on the seat in front of you. When you stand up, pulling on the seat in front of you annoys the person in that seat. If their seat tilts back too far and blocks your way, politely ask that person to please return his seat to the upright position so you may exit.

Make sure you talk softly when people around you are trying to sleep.

You might be more comfortable taking off your shoes and wearing socks during a night flight. I sure hope your socks are clean.

Keep the volume turned down on your headset so as not to disturb your neighbors.

Keep your conversation soft and sweet. During a flight is not the time to discuss the latest plane crash or how a friend of yours became airsick.

Keep your arms and legs out of the aisle. You could embarrass yourself by tripping someone. The other person might become seriously hurt.

GOOD-BYE!

Gather all of your belongings.

Wait patiently in line to deplane.

Thank the crew as you leave. "I enjoyed the flight. Thank you." "Nice landing, Captain." Remember to look into the eyes of the crew members rather than the ground.

BAGGAGE CLAIM

Be prepared to show your claim tickets to the security guard at the exit. Some airports do not allow you to leave with your luggage until they know that your claim tickets match the numbers on the suitcase tickets.

The hardest part of traveling is not the packing or the flying. It's the frustration over finding your car in the parking lot. Good luck!

AUTOMOBILE

Automobiles were so strange in the late 19th century that circuses displayed them. Today, millions of cars transport people from one place to another.

Car trips can be fun or a real bore. Good planning is the key to an enjoyable car trip.

PLAN OF ACTION

Make a list of activities you can enjoy in the car -- a lap craft, games, books, tape player with headset, and pad and pencil.

Keep your activities in a bag or box so they do not become scattered all over the car.

Ask the driver to mark the trip route on a map of your own so you can follow the progress of the trip. Then you will not continually ask, "Are we there yet?" "How much longer?" These questions only make the trip drag on for everyone.

STAY OUT!

Never ride in a car with someone who has been drinking. Drunk drivers aren't able to quickly respond to an emergency and could cause an accident. If you take a chance, it will probably be your last ride. Statistics prove it. If you doubt these, then call or write to M.A.D.D. (Mothers Against Drunk Driving) at 1-800-438-6233 or 699 Airport Freeway, Suite 310, Hurst, TX 76053.

Anger and automobiles don't mix. Dr. John Schowalter, the president of the American Academy of Child and Adolescent Psychiatry, says that anger is the leading cause of car accidents, second only to drugs and alcohol. Cool down before you even think of driving a car or riding with a "hot head".

Avoid hitchhiking. Catching rides with strangers can be dangerous.

BUCKLE UP

Wearing a seat belt is not only smart but is the law in many states.

BE A CONSIDERATE PASSENGER

Distracting the driver is not only discourteous but dangerous. He or she needs to keep both hands and eyes on the road.

When you stop for gas, use the restroom. Then the driver will not have to make a special stop for you.

Keep your trash in a litter bag rather than throwing it all over the car or out the window.

Keep your head and arms in the car.

Traveling by automobile offers a great opportunity to become better acquainted with your fellow passengers, including your family. With no outside distractions, you can have a good time sharing thoughts, ideas, and dreams. Turn off the radio, occasionally, and enjoy one another's company.

BUS

Traveling by bus is slow, so most people prefer to make long trips by car or plane. The bus is a great way, however, to travel around a city or to and from school or work. Some buses carry as few as eight people while larger buses can transport more than seventy people.

Have your ticket or money ready as you enter the bus. Ask the driver if eating is permissible. Find a seat quickly. Do not make any loud or sudden noises that will distract the bus driver

When riding on a city bus, give your seat to an elderly person or mother with small children. No matter how tired, standing on a moving bus is still easier for a younger person.

Thank the bus driver when you exit the bus. "Thank you. Have a nice day."

TRAIN

Train travel, no longer the most popular mode of travel for people, still transports products such as lumber, coal, grain and machinery. Many people desire to reach their destinations quickly so they choose traveling by air.

For short trips within a city and the surrounding suburbs, people use commuter trains. The same etiquette applies as on city buses.

Train travel can be a fun adventure and a good way to see the countryside. Sitting in a coach car, the economical way to travel, offers little service. Some people choose to pay to use the dining car and sleeping cars.

Trains have limited space, so limit your little luggage. Also, do not spread your belongings all over the train. Keep your area tidy, with all trash picked up.

The diner car is a restaurant on the train. Not everyone on the train can eat at once. Do not linger after a meal. Other passengers would like to eat.

The seats in the observation car sit up higher than the coach seats. This car has a glass bubble dome, making viewing of the surroundings easy and delightful. Not everyone on the train can fit into this car, so take turns.

TAKING TRIPS

Practice good manners away from home as well as in your own community. Think of yourself as an ambassador to your city, state, and even your country when traveling. People you meet will form their opinions of your part of the country by your actions. If you are kind and well-mannered, they will think of your area as a friendly place to live.

Don't call attention to your self in the way you dress. Dress modestly and appropriately for your activities and the area you are visiting.

Don't call attention to yourself by talking loudly or being demanding. A smile and a little patience will take you far.

257

Have fun without calling attention to yourself. You can laugh without becoming undignified.

Unfortunately, some Americans have given the United States a bad name. They travel through a foreign country without bothering to become familiar with the customs of that particular area. People judge them as rude and loud.

Some tourists do not bother to become acquainted with the local people. They do not even take a few seconds to exchange pleasantries. "The mountains in your country are beautiful and the people so friendly." Some foreigners will judge all Americans as unfriendly for one person's negative comment or rude behavior. Prove them wrong!

Before you visit a foreign country, visit your local library or bookstore. Your vacation will be more rewarding by taking the time to learn about the history, culture, climate, area, and activities of that particular country.

> My husband, daughter, and I enjoyed several meals in a beautiful mansion in England several years ago. During our first meal in the dining room, I commented, "Listen to all of the laughter, conversation, and clanging of silverware. We haven't heard such a lively group of diners in all of England." My husband replied, "Look around. We are eating with all Americans." In the country inns and private homes we had dined in, the silence was almost deafening. You could hear a knife placed upon a plate.

Britons enjoy a quiet atmosphere during a meal. Some visitors might be insensitive to this way of eating. They might speak and laugh loudly, offending the people of the host country. Study up on local etiquette. Be a considerate visitor.

258

DOORS, ELEVATORS, ESCALATORS

DOORS

We pass through doors countless times a day without giving much thought to our actions. Here are some guidelines for safety and to make you feel more comfortable in public.

Pass through a door with grace. Don't barge through a door, slamming it against the wall. You might damage the wall or may hit someone standing on the other side. After you pass through the doorway, turn and gently close the door. Keep your hand on the doorknob rather than slamming it closed.

As you pass through a push door, check to see if someone is behind you. Many times someone in front of me has let go of the door. If I had not quickly stuck my hand out, the door would have slammed in my face. How polite to stand and hold a door open for someone behind you.

Allow an adult to pass through a door before you. A lady passes through before a gentleman. If the door is heavy and swings away from you, it would make more sense for the gentleman to pass through and hold the door open for the lady.

Don't get "hung up" with revolving doors. Some men find it easier to push the door from behind the lady. Other gentlemen prefer to enter the revolving door first, waiting for the lady on the street side. Be a lady and leave the decision up to the gentleman.

ELEVATORS

Common sense usually dictates rules of etiquette when riding elevators. Whether you decided to enter or exit first or last, be patient and courteous.

A gentleman allows a lady to exit an elevator first so he can hold the door open for her. If a lady is in the back of a crowded elevator, common sense would tell the gentleman in front to exit first.

259

A Real Gentleman

When you see elevator doors about to close, please do not shout, "Hold it!" Neither should you stick your arm between the closing doors. Wait patiently for the next elevator.

Before entering an elevator, stand back and allow people to exit first.

The person standing by the button panel in the elevator holds the "Door Open" button until people have exited and entered.

If you are alone on an elevator and a man enters, leave immediately if you feel uncomfortable. The next elevator will be by in a few seconds.

Keep conversations on elevators to a minimum. People feel awkward about everyone being able to hear their conversation. If you do talk, speak softly.

As you exit the elevator, remember to say, "Please excuse me," if you have to get around someone. People are willing to move out of the way when someone is courteous. They appreciate a smile and a "Thank you," as well.

ESCALATORS

When offered a choice, I often opt for taking the stairs over riding an escalator for added exercise. But the "moving stairs" was the greatest invention for tired feet and shoppers carrying a bundle of packages.

For safety, hold on to the handrail and face forward. When you exit, move quickly to the side so someone quickly trying to pass you does not knock into you.

MORE HELPFUL HINTS

♠ Travel agents are free and will help you plan your trip.

♠ Do not take more clothes than you need. Hauling around a lot of suitcases is no fun. You can wear the same outfit more than once.

♠ Plastic bags are great organizers. Take extra bags along. You will find many uses for them.

♠ Two of your best travel companions will be your travel iron and a small flashlight.

♠ Carry two sets of names and addresses of people you may need to contact on your trip and back home. Put one list in your wallet and one in your suitcase. Wallets, purses, and luggage occasionally become lost or stolen. You might need the backup list.

♠ Parking lot tip: The minute you park, write the location on a piece of paper to tuck in your wallet. By recording the exact location, you will save anxious moments searching for your car. Be sure to leave the parking lot ticket in your car. If you take your ticket with you and lose it, you will have to pay a maximum fee to retrieve your car.

REVIEW
Out And About

1. On the beach, be aware of running too closely to sunbathers. You could kick _____ on them. ("Beach And Pool")

2. Rather than chatting with a family member or friend, how should you enter a church? ("Church") _____

3. Why should hospital visitors be quiet in the halls? ("Hospital Visitor")

_____

4. Is the library a good place for quiet conversations with friends? ("Library") Yes or No

5. Some guests sleep during the day so _____ and _____ quietly in the halls. ("Motels And Hotels")

6. When you arrive to a movie before your friends, may you save a place in line for them? ("Movies") Yes or No

7. What is some dressing room etiquette? ("Shopping")

_____

8. What is something that annoys another spectator at a sporting event? ("Sporting Events") _____

9. When attending a ballet, concert, or play, does the lady or the gentlemen follow the usher with the other to follow? ("Theatre") Hint: This guideline applies to following a waitress or waiter in a restaurant, too.

_____

10. Under "Other Considerations," what are two other ways of showing courtesy on a flight? ("Transportation: Air")   a)_____
_____ b) _____

11. As you pass through a push door, how can you extend courtesy to the person behind you? ("Doors") _____

12. Does a lady or a gentleman exit an elevator first? ("Elevators") _____

Dear Parent,

"Out and About" takes the guess work out of how to behave in public places. Explanations follow the guidelines so your son or daughter can understand why rules make for a more pleasant atmosphere.

He will learn to respect and appreciate the quiet surroundings in a library and museum. She will relax when attending a concert, knowing when and how to move about. Rather than focusing on playing on the elevator or roaming and laughing through the halls, your child will concentrate on spreading sunshine when he visits a friend in the hospital. Traveling will become more enjoyable when your child learns consideration for fellow passengers.

Practice reinforces knowledge. After you read a section with your son or daughter, participate in that activity together. Read about visiting a museum and then go to one together and practice the rules of etiquette. Visit someone in the hospital following the guidelines presented in this chapter. Ride a city bus and quietly prompt your son or daughter to give up his or her seat to an older person.

Encourage your son or daughter to show consideration to others. Whether people compliment on good manners or not (but they will!), your son or daughter will gain a deep satisfaction in knowing that he/she is making the world a more desirable place in which to live.

Deborah Wuerslin

LIFE LINE
Implementing Excellence

Public Speaking

Let your conversation be gracious as well as sensible, for then you will have the right answer for everyone.
Colossians 4:6 Living Bible

Whatever is in the heart overflows into speech.
Luke 6:45 NIV

Let your manner of life be worthy of the gospel of Christ.
Philippians 1:27 RSV

Think of an effective public speaker you personally know. They are rare, unfortunately, but there are some who are exceptional. Perhaps you enjoy listening to one of your teachers or your principal. Maybe your pastor holds your attention. A local politician or an actor might captivate you.

What draws you to your favorites? They probably speak clearly and with sincerity. They use gestures and put expression in their voices. Their eye contact personalizes their dialogue or speech. Visualize and imitate these qualities.

How do these people express themselves in private situations? As you master skills in public speaking, ask the Lord to help you communicate effectively wherever you may be and whomever you are with. May the content of your words as well as your delivery always be pleasing to your Father above.

The brain is a wonderful thing. It never stops functioning from the time you're born until the moment you stand up to make a speech.
-Unknown

PUBLIC SPEAKING

Learning proper techniques to speaking in front of others may not eliminate all of your anxieties, but you will be able to speak more easily. Practice makes perfect. If you want to be a better public speaker, you need to give more speeches using the following guidelines.

KNOW YOUR AUDIENCE

Will you be speaking to fellow students, adults and parents at a P.T.A. meeting, a church group, or your tennis club? Your speech should be at the level of your audience. Just as you would not talk baby talk at a P.T.A. meeting, you would not want to get too technical in front of young people. Write your speech according to your audience.

DRESS ACCORDINGLY

Be neat and clean. Do not wear anything that will attract undo attention to your outfit and take away from what you are trying to say. Remember to dress for the occasion. You would wear a more casual outfit when speaking in front of your class than you would at a P.T.A. meeting or a banquet. Jewelry must not make any noise, including watches that beep.

PREPARE AND PRACTICE

Write out your speech, making sure that the grammar is correct and the content is in a logical order with a beginning, middle, and ending. Rehearse your speech many times while standing. Practice moving your head around as though you were looking at different people. Then write a short outline on index cards. Now practice giving the speech by occasionally glancing at your outline.

APPROACHING THE SPEAKER'S PLATFORM

Remember your body language. Approach the speaker's platform as a poised young woman or gentleman of confidence. Even if you are nervous, do not let anyone know. If you announce your nervousness either by telling your audience or through your body language, they will look for signs of anxiety throughout your entire speech. A smile will put your audience at ease as well as make you feel more relaxed.

DON'T TELL

If you did not prepare well for your speech or do not completely understand your subject matter, do not tell your audience. If you make excuses, they will spend their time listening for mistakes.

RELAXING TECHNIQUES

Before I speak, I take a few deep breaths. I also tighten my hands in fists and then relax them.

SLOW START

Your audience will take a minute or two to get used to you, the way you look and the sound of your voice, so do not jump into the meat of the subject matter right away. Start with greeting your audience and any special guests.

POSTURE

Remember how to stand properly. Your hands can either hold your notecards, rest on the podium (not grab) or hang down at your sides. Do not play with your hands. If you do, your audience will focus on your hands. Hide them behind your back if you cannot keep them still.

EYE CONTACT

You will catch your audience yawning if you don't make, at least occasional, eye contact.

WATER

If you are going to speak for any length of time, have a glass of water nearby. Drink some water before you speak, as well.

GUM AND CANDY

Only your teeth and tongue should be in your mouth when giving a speech. Chewing gum or sucking on candy will make it difficult for you to pronounce your words correctly. Besides, ladies and gentlemen do not chew gum.

YOUR VOICE

Always talk directly into the microphone. Speak clearly and be careful not to shout and blast out your audience. If there is no microphone, make sure that you speak so that the person farthest away from you can hear you. When you keep your head up, your audience will hear you more easily. Do not speak with a flat voice. Use expression.

COUGHING AND SNEEZING

Excuse yourself and turn your head to cough, sneeze, or blow your nose. Sometimes speakers will blow their nose or take a drink of water just before making a dramatic point. The pause adds suspense.

DRAWING A BLANK

If your mind suddenly goes blank, do not panic. Pause in silence rather than filling in with "Um." Use this as an excuse to get a drink of water.

THE END

Good speeches often fizzle out because they end too abruptly or are too drawn out. Summarize quickly and than make a point that the audience will take home and think about. Finish talking before you start to move away. Say "Thank you" with a smile and then walk away with poise.

REVIEW
Public Speaking

1. Why is the way you dress and accessorize your outfit so important when speaking in public?

_____

2. Practice your speech from the entire copy. Then write a short _____ on index cards. Practice from the cards and only glance occasionally at your notes.

3. Don't announce to the audience you are _____. Wear a big _____ and your audience will relax and enjoy your speech.

4. Why should you not jump into the subject matter right away?

_____

5. What should you do with your hands if you have no note cards, podium, or microphone to hold on to? _____

_____

6. If you are shy, should you look above everyone's head during your speech? Yes or No

7. Speak clearly and use _____ rather than speaking in a flat voice.

8. Speech ticks often appear when you pause. Rather than saying, "Um," what can you do? _____

_____

9. The _____ of a speech is just as important as the beginning.

10. Finish _____ before you walk away. When you end, pause, say "_____" with a *smile* and *eye contact* and then walk away.

Dear Parent,

After evening storytime and prayers, our children took turns in leading songs to the rest of the family. As a toddler, one of them just stood in front of us and shyly smiled as we helped him select a song to sing. As time passed, he picked his own songs but still remained a silent song leader. Eventually his confidence grew and he actually led in the singing each time his turn would come up. He became comfortable with standing in front of our family -- a beginning.

By the time our children started giving oral book reports in school, they gave the appearance of being experienced public speakers. Although not polished and at times nervous, they knew how to send positive signals to their audience.

Show and tell time does not have to wait for the classroom. Motivate your son or daughter to share hobbies, events, stories, and jokes with you, standing in front of you as he/she would on stage or in front of a class.

A speaker often focuses totally on his speech content, excluding style of presentation. This chapter concentrates on teaching your son or daughter how to project a positive image. He/she will learn to capture the audience's attention even if the subject matter does not sound interesting.

Help your son/daughter rehearse his/her oral book reports, speeches, and parts in plays following the guidelines in this chapter. Confidence will grow out of practice and positive reinforcement.

Deborah Wuerslin

LIFE LINE
Implementing Excellence

Working With Class

Trust in the Lord with all your heart and lean not on your own understanding; in all your ways acknowledge him, and he will make your paths straight.
Proverbs 3:5,6 NIV

Let everyone be sure that he is doing his very best, for then he will have the personal satisfaction of work well done, and won't need to compare himself with someone else.
Galatians 6:4 Living Bible

Often we make our own plans and then ask God to bless them. Praying before you make any decisions can save you from learning some hard lessons. You might find yourself in a job you do not enjoy or in a relationship that you wish you could change.

Perhaps you did pray for guidance before your boss hired you. If your job doesn't seem suitable for you, ask the Lord for advice. He may be trying to speak to you. He *promises* to guide you in all things. You ask and He will begin to work in your situation as and where you are.

A boss is willing to teach you job duties, but he does not expect to teach character qualities such as friendliness, honesty, dependability, and punctuality. When you look at any job as an opportunity to serve, your humble spirit will enable you to serve others well.

In theatre, there is a saying, "There are no small parts, only small actors." Your work reflects on your character and attitude. No matter the task, or whether or not you are paid for the job, work for the Lord. He is your true boss. Give Him your best. Serve Him with excellence.

The most important quality in an employee is not skill; it is character. A man of good character can acquire skill; a man without good character rarely becomes a desirable and profitable employee in a legitimate business.
--C.E. Bernard

WORKING WITH CLASS

> During a bus ride home from school one afternoon, Diane's two closest friends, Laura and Laurie, grilled her on her success as a baby-sitter. They wanted to know why her neighbors asked her to care for their children more often than any other teenager in the neighborhood. Diane was not sure why they picked her, so she decided to ask some of the parents.
> "You are trustworthy" replied Mrs. Johnson. "You follow every instruction I give you." "You come to play with my children, rather than to sit in front of the television" answered Mrs. Gelaude. Mrs. Isaac also liked that Diane helped her little girl to pick up toys and to clean up any mess she made in the kitchen when getting a snack. Mrs. Castleberry appreciated the good example that Diane set by being well-mannered and having a neat appearance. If Diane had to cancel a job due to illness, she did her best to help find a dependable substitute.

> Paul and Mark Thomas gained a reputation in their neighborhood for their first-rate lawn and yard care service. Mrs. Stine never had to ask these hard-working boys to repeat a job. They strived for excellence in every task performed. The Billingslys appreciated Paul and Mark's dependability. They did not have to call and remind them to mow their lawn every week. The boys were also sharp to perform tasks without being asked. Other neighbors respected them for not socializing with friends while working and for not playing loud music. They took care of their equipment by using it safely, cleaning it off, and putting it away.

Regardless of the job, you build a reputation for how you work. Earn the respect of your employer and peers for being dependable, honest, and cooperative.

"Working with Class" will assist you in securing that desired job. You will please your employers. You'll get repeat jobs, referrals, and personal pleasure from your efforts.

WHAT CAN I DO?

List on a sheet of paper your interests, skills and talents, and job training. Do you enjoy working around people or by yourself? Indoors or outdoors? Do you enjoy working with children, adults, or the elderly? How about animals?

Example 1:

INTERESTS	SKILLS & TALENTS	JOB TRAINING
Children	Singing	Baby-sitting
Indoors/Outdoors	Ballet and Tap	Public Speaking Course
Variety of Jobs (nothing repetitious)	Cartoon Drawing	Red Cross Lifesaving
Enjoy Teaching	Sewing	
Skiing, Track	Cooking	
Camping, Hiking		
Tennis		
Swimming		

This individual might enjoy becoming a summer camp counselor, day care worker, or starting a party planning/entertainment business. Sewing skills are helpful to customers in a fabric store. Organize a children's theatre group and put on an end-of-summer play. Parents would help with costumes and sets as well as pay you for your directing/drama teaching.

Example 2:

INTERESTS	SKILLS & TALENTS	JOB TRAINING
Alone or with people	Good in Math	Yard Care
Outdoors/Camping,/ Sports	Athletic	Babysitting
Machinery/Architect	Hard Worker	Helped Dad fix tools
Animals	Handyman	Basic Woodworking
Reading	Eagle Scout	Household Chores

This individual might enjoy yard and house maintenance work. Assisting a construction crew would sharpen building skills and increase an interest in architecture. Working at a sport's camp would put those athletic skills to use. Helping in a veterinarian's office would be enjoyable for an animal lover.

Your parents, teachers, and a school counselor can give you ideas for a job that suits you. They might also be a resource for ideas as to where to look for a job. Perhaps they have some connections. It's still true that who you know is as important as what you know.

Here are some suggestions to get you started:
Baby-sitting, children's summer theatre group, companion to a shut-in, car washing, errand service (you might need a car or bike for this service), housecleaning, music lessons, party planning, party assistant, party entertainer (clown, dancer, magician, singer), pet care (grooming, exercising, baby-sitting), plant care (especially when neighbors are away on vacation), tutoring (school work), yard care (lawn mowing, weeding, watering), raking leaves, shoveling snow-filled sidewalks, window washing.

Sixteen year olds can apply for jobs in businesses such as fast-food restaurants, grocery stores, department stores, restaurants, beauty shops, florists, and hotels as bellhops.

Decide whether earning money or learning a skill is the most important. Working for a savings and loan as an errand boy, helping at a construction site, or assisting a veterinarian may pay less than other part-time jobs. The experience and knowledge, however, may prove more beneficial.

GETTING READY FOR THE INTERVIEW
Making a positive first impression increases your chances in securing the job you desire. For the young person looking for baby-sitting, lawn mowing jobs, or pet care, print note cards. I call these "INDEX RESUMES." The index card will tell your prospective customers a little bit about you and your job experience and service. Print these cards neatly in ink or use a typewriter.

Typical cards look like these:

Job Desired: BABY-SITTING

Jennifer Tota, age 13
3107 Workers Lane
Challenge, Georgia 30000
926-0000

Baby-sitting fee: Minimum: $ x.xx/hr.
Experience: --Baby-sitter for one year.
    --Volunteer at local school for the blind.
    --Experience taking care of baby brother.
    --Volunteer at local nursing home.
References: --Mr. and Mrs. Jeff Smith, 926-0000
     --Ms. Joyce Burnett, 926-0000
     --Rev. Clyde Wiley, 926-0000

Job Desired: Lawn Care

Ryan Conboy, age 13
231 Mountain Drive
Juniper, Colorado 80824
468-0000

Description of services:
  --Mow lawn, bag, rake leaves & grass, edge, trim,
    sweep, weed, water lawn and flower beds.
  --Provide all supplies except bags for grass
    clippings.
  --Will water yard & house plants during vacations.
References:
  --Mr. & Mrs. Bob Crutchfield, 469-0000
  --Mr. & Mrs. John Sharp, 469-0000

Don't hand out your index resumes randomly. Ask your parents and other adults you know for names of families for whom you might enjoy working. Ask permission before using anyone's name as a reference. Don't use a family member as a reference.

INDEX RESUMES are more effective when delivered in person. Dress in a sharp-looking casual outfit, clean and neatly pressed. Introduce yourself as you hand the card to them, making eye contact and wearing a

275

smile. "Hello. My name is _____. I baby-sit (or pet-sit...) and would like to offer my services. Here is my resume. My phone number is included." Whether interviewed or not, thank the person for his or her time.

They will be impressed that you took the time to tell them a little bit about yourself. They will appreciate the references you gave him to check out your performance on previous jobs and your character (likeable, honest, trustworthy, ...).

A regular RESUME is typed on 8 1/2" x 11" paper. A resume is a summation of your education, job experience, and interests and hobbies. Keep your resume short and concise. You can elaborate during your interview. For each job, give a brief description of your duties. Also give each employer's address and phone number.

RESUME

JOHN MICHAEL

JOB OBJECTIVE
Veterinary Assistant

PERSONAL DATA   Address: 2121 Anywhere Street
                         Atlanta, Georgia 30058
Telephone: (404) 985-0000
Marital Status: Single
Date of Birth: 28 December 1975
Health: Excellent, Height 5'11", Weight 155 lbs.
Hobbies: Skiing, Camping, Tennis, Reading, Bicycling, Pet
        Care
School Activities: Marching and Concert Band, 1989, 1990
Junior Varsity Soccer, 1990, 1991
Varsity Soccer, 1992, 1993
Yearbook Staff, 1992
German Club, 1991, 1992, 1993
Beta Club, 1990
National Honor Society, 1991-1993

EDUCATION
        June 1993 graduate Shiloh High School, with honors

EXPERIENCE
        Cashier, Kroger, 1992, 1993
                Cashier and occasional stock boy
        Lawn and Yard Care, 1987-present
                Mowed neighbor lawns, prepared beds for planting,weeded,
                Watered yards during neighbor's absence
        Pet Care, 1987 - 1992
                Fed and exercised pets for vacationing neighbors, clipped
                toenails on dogs and rabbits
        Summer Camp Counselor, 1989 - 1991
                Supervised assigned campers in their activities, taught
                canoeing, and organized parent night

REFERENCES

Mr. Brian Michael, Kroger Manager
Kroger
3026 Granite Boulevard, Stone Mountain, GA 30087
(400) 469-0000

Mr. and Mrs. Eric Christopher, Scoutmaster Troop 40
3020 Riverview Way, Stone Mountain, GA 30087
(400) 498-0000

Mr. and Mrs. Christopher Whyte
6161 Academy Drive, Annistown, GA 30057
(400) 985-0000

Reverend Clyde Wiley
Church of the Redeemer,
41 Agape Way, Annistown, GA 30057
(400) 985-0000

Show the employer your organizational skills. Bring your own pen for filling out the application. Carry your resume with you even if you apply at a fast-food restaurant or department store for a part-time job. Having your resume on hand makes filling out the job application an easier task.

COVER LETTER

Include a cover letter with your resume. The cover letter introduces you to the company or person with whom you are seeking employment. An interesting cover letter makes the reader curious enough to read your resume.

Include any information pertaining to the job you are applying for. For example, mention your experience with pet care if applying for a job at a veterinary office. Mention how you heard about the job you are applying for: the newspaper, a customer or employee, or a friend of the employer.

1257 Willow Avenue
San Diego, California 92122
April 4, 1993

Mrs. Erin Nichole
Manager
Kelly's Apparel
31 Business Parkway
San Diego, California 92122

Dear Mrs. Nichole,

One of your sales clerks, Caroline Veith, suggested I contact you about a possible job opening as sales clerk next month. Mrs. Veith has become a friend of my family during the five years we have shopped at Kelly's Apparel.

I am a senior at Ocean High School and will be graduating in five weeks. Because I shop at Kelly's Apparel so frequently, I am familiar with the layout of the store and a knowledge of your operation. The friendly, prompt, and courteous service has always impressed me. These, too, are my work skills.

My sewing skills will enable me to better assist your customers because of my knowledge of design, color, and fit.

As a hospital volunteer for two years, I accepted tasks that were sometimes unpleasant but very necessary. I can assure you I am a hard worker and very dependable. References for my past jobs, volunteer work, school and church activities are attached.

Please contact me any afternoon after 4:00 p.m. for an interview at 985-0000. Mrs. Nichole, I look forward to hearing from you.

Sincerely,

Kerry Diann Williams

APPLICATION INFORMATION

In order to completely fill out a job application, gather the following and place it in a folder. Take the folder with you to the place of business. Be prepared and organized.

- Most applications ask you to list your education -- schools attended, addresses, time periods, and grades completed. (Your background)
- Former jobs and work experience.
- Volunteer work in your community and church.
- You may need proof of your age -- birth certificate or driver's license.
- A social security number.
- List of references other than relatives who the company can call to verify your job experience and character. Ask permission before listing someone as a reference. Some applications ask you to list at least one person who has known you for more than ten years. Have names, addresses, and phone numbers of your references with you. You may use names of former employers, neighbors, teachers, or a pastor.

THE INTERVIEW

An interview works both ways. The employer checks you out, and you evaluate your future boss and the company or place of business.

TWO'S A CROWD

Go to your interview alone. Your parents or friends do not tag along.

BE PUNCTUAL

The interviewer will judge a late appearance as a possible bad habit on the job.

DRESS FOR THE OCCASION

Casual clothes are not appropriate except when applying for manual labor jobs (mechanic, construction worker, ...). Avoid wild styles. Dress conservatively. A semiformal dress or tuxedo would be overdressing.

Instead, ladies wear a skirt and blouse, suit, or a dress you would wear to church. Gentlemen, a shirt and tie with nice pants are in order. Be neat, clean, and polish those shoes. Leave your gum at home. Many employers do not tolerate over-sized earrings or extreme makeup applications.

Dress in the same manner when merely dropping by to pick up an application. You might be granted an interview on the spot! It happens frequently.

GOOD MANNERS make a good impression. Be prepared to shake the interviewer's hand when you enter his office. Wear a smile and use eye contact. After the interviewer invites you to sit down (not until then), remember your posture. Good posture reflects confidence. Do not place anything nor read anything on the interviewer's desk.

BE TRUTHFUL

Answer all questions honestly.

Be prepared to answer questions concerning your extra curricular activities, grades in school, and how often you miss school (Remember, your employer can check with your school for verification.). An employer judges a future employee partly on his school performance. A student with good grades knows the value of hard work. A student involved in sports, school and church activities is outgoing. A student who does not miss much school is dependable.

Explain how qualities developed on previous paid or volunteer jobs are assets you can apply to your new job. Working in a nursing home, for example, required a great deal of patience. You also learned flexibility when communicating to the elderly. Some understood verbal communication while others only understood facial expression and hand guidance. Perhaps your hospital work required an occasional unpleasant duty, so you are capable of performing undesirable tasks as well as those you enjoy. Your lawn mowing jobs taught you to work thoroughly and quickly, so your employers would recommend you for other jobs.

Tell the interviewer if a boss ever left you alone on a job so he will know that he can count on you to work when unsupervised.

Relate how you coped with a difficult job experience. Perhaps a child on a baby-sitting job became ill. Rather than struggling, you reached out for help and called a neighbor since you could not contact the parents. The interviewer will discover you are not afraid to ask for help and you do not fold under pressure.

An employer might ask, "Do you like yourself?" He realizes that a good-natured employee makes customers and fellow employees happy.

Be prepared to tell the interviewer one of your best qualities. Relate your response to the job for which you are applying. If the job requires working with people, mention your ability to get along with others.

If asked to state a bad habit or character flaw, mention only something not related to the job. If the job involves working with machines, do not say that machines intimidate you. You could say you bite your fingernails. A better response is, "I have a habit of expecting perfection in my work, and I can become frustrated. But I am working on striving for excellence rather than perfection."

Other questions an interviewer might ask:
- What courses in school did you enjoy the most? The least?
- What were your extracurricular activities?
- How do you relax?
- What do you want to do five years from now? Ten years?
- Who are you role models?
- How did former bosses treat you?
- Why have you chosen our company?

BE DIRECT AND CONCISE
Do not ramble or become sidetracked when answering questions. Stay focused.

STAND BY YOUR CONVICTIONS
An interviewer might debate your answers just to test your convictions on a given topic.

REMAIN CALM
When asked a difficult question, don't rush your answer. Give a well thought-out response, and then stand by your answer.

To test for stress, an interviewer might allow long periods of silence. A confident person will not become fidgety nor will he change his answer out of nervousness.

BE LOYAL
Do not speak badly of a former boss or a negative work experience.

TAKE TURNS
Ask questions about the company. Hopefully, you researched the company and can express the qualities and goals with which you identify. Make sure you do not confuse labels and slogans with other companies. When applying at McDonald's, make sure you mention you like "Big Macs" and not "Whoppers."

Ask about job responsibilities and opportunities for advancement. Ask about salary or vacation time only after the interviewer hires you.

THANK YOU
Send a thank-you note, thanking the interviewer for his or her time and kindness.

> How disappointing to learn that I was not hired for a job I had interviewed for as a 19 year old. I wrote a thank-you note anyway. One year later, the company that had turned me down, called and offered me a job. They told me they did not have a vacancy the previous year, but my file showed my interview was impressive. My thank-you note for the interview had been attached to my application.

EMPLOYEE EXCELLENCE
A good employee is friendly, cheerful, and helpful.

Lending A Helping Hand

The Unreliable Employee

TOP-NOTCH EMPLOYEE

- Arrives on the job a few minutes early, becoming settled and ready to start on time. An employee is considered late when walking through the door at the appointed starting time.

- Reads related work material handed out concerning job responsibilities, safety rules, benefits.

- Follows the rules and guidelines of the employer.

- Maintains a neat appearance.

- Focuses on work and saves socializing for breaks.

- Does not gossip.

- Asks intelligent questions and listens to the answers.

- Asks for help or further instructions rather than repeating mistakes. Remembers to say thank you.

- Completes a job before leaving. Leaving an unfinished letter in the typewriter or sweeping half a floor because the work day ended makes bosses unhappy.

- Willing to stay late once in a while.

- Willing to perform a task other than the assigned job description.

- Lends a helping hand to fellow workers.

- Works efficiently.

- Friendly to co-workers as well as management and customers.

- Wears a smile and makes eye contact when speaking to someone.

- Shows interest in fellow workers. "I heard you talk to someone about tennis. Do you play on a team?" or "You wear some of the cutest clothes. Where did you learn to sew so beautifully?"

- Does not display a temper to an obnoxious customer.

- Occasionally brightens up the office or store with flowers or homemade goodies.

> An owner of a fast-food restaurant in Atlanta looks for personality when hiring. He employs someone who can create a pleasant atmosphere. He realizes customers return to his restaurant for fast, friendly service more than for the good food he serves.

SECOND-RATE EMPLOYEE

- Asks for help before trying to solve the problem on his/her own.

- Laughs at other's ideas.

- Never apologizes for mistakes.

- Talks to fellow employees without showing interest to customers.

- Speaks to customers or fellow workers in a loud tone.

- Has a know-it-all attitude and brags about his/her skills.

- Tells a customer, "I can't help you; I'm on break."

- Moves slowly when performing a task.

- Calls in sick when doesn't feel like working.

- Eats food or licks fingers on the job.

- Steals paper, pencils, and other items from his/her place of employment.

- Uses the copier machine for personal business.

- Makes phone calls other than during breaks.

- Dresses immodestly or inappropriately for the job.

- Uses bad language.

- Complains and criticizes the boss and fellow workers.

- Complains about the company in front of customers.

Acquiring new skills and meeting new people enhances your life. Make your job a pleasant learning experience. Devote your work time to your assigned tasks, pursuing excellence. Even small jobs should receive your best efforts. Earn respect from your boss and fellow workers by working diligently.

Creating a pleasant atmosphere at your place of employment brings you the satisfaction of brightening the lives of others. You will easily find a job when you gain a reputation for your loyalty, dependability, honesty, and cooperative and friendly character.

Happy job hunting! You are now prepared to work with class.

REVIEW
Working With Class

1. The most important quality in an employee is not _____ it is
_____.

2. List three areas of interest in your life and three skills or talents. ("What
Can I DO?")   1.   1.
                        2.   2.
                        3.   3.

3. What summer job could you use your skills or talents in an area that
interests you?

_____

4. What information does an index resume include?

_____

5. How is a regular resume different from an index resume? List three
differences.
        a)
        b)
        c)

6. What is the purpose of a cover letter?_____

7. What information should you take with you when applying for a job?
Briefly list all six. ("Application Information")
        a)
        b)
        c)
        d)
        e)
        f)

8. To make a good first impression, how should you dress for an interview (including when you pick up an application)?

_____

9. When you first meet your interviewer you should:
                    a)
                    b)
                    c)
                    d)

10. Be prepared to answer questions concerning:
                    a)
                    b)
                    c)

11. If the interviewer asks you to share a bad habit, what should you *not* say?

_____

12. What should you send the interviewer after you return home?

_____

13. A top-notch employee focuses on work and saves socializing for

_____

14. A top-notch employee will perform a task other than _____

_____

15. A second-rate employee talks to fellow employees without showing interest to _____.

16. Should an employee share negatives about his company with customers?
                    Yes or No

17. What does a second-rate employee do about the boss and fellow workers?

_____

18. Who should you go to with a problem about your job or a fellow employee? (Remember to pray first so you share in the right attitude.)

_____

Dear Parent,

Employers look for character qualities such as honesty, dependability, loyalty, punctuality, and friendliness. Most employers are willing to teach skills to untrained workers but do not expect to focus all of their energy in character-building lessons. Teach your son or daughter positive character qualities as you assign responsibilities around the home. Encourage dependability, for example, in taking out the trash on pick-up days without needing a reminder. Teach punctuality for feeding pets. Praise a positive and cooperative work attitude, always ready to pitch in and help another family member. Instill job excellence by teaching your son or daughter to complete every task to the best of his/her ability.

Frequently remind your son or daughter how positive work traits help create a more pleasant atmosphere in the home. Relate these qualities to present and future jobs outside the home.

"Just as you ask us for help when you experience difficulty with a task, a future boss of yours will appreciate your desire to get the job done correctly." "Mrs. Anders appreciates your dependability in following her instructions when caring for her children." "The Goods said they are grateful for your honesty for giving them the wallet you found in their yard while you were raking their leaves." "Thank you for beginning the job at the time your mother and I asked you to start. You know, someday you will have a boss who will appreciate your punctuality."

Everyone benefits when your son or daughter works with class.

Deborah Wuerslin

Index